Olympic
Architecture
2000
Building Sydney

Olympic
Architecture
Building Sydney

2000

Patrick Bingham-Hall

The Watermark Press

First published in 1999
by The Watermark Press
Sydney, Australia

The publishers would like to acknowledge the considerable support of
Payce Consolidated and Leighton Contractors in making this publication possible.

Contributing Writers:
    Patrick Bingham-Hall
    Philip Goad,
    Harry Margalit
    Paul McGillick,
    Chris Johnson
    Bridget Smyth

The National Library of Australia
Cataloguing-in-Publication data:

Bingham-Hall, Patrick
Olympic Architecture: Building Sydney 2000

Includes index.
ISBN 0 949284 39 4.

1. Olympic Games (27th : 2000 : Sydney, N.S.W.) - Pictorial works. 2. Olympic
Games 27th : 2000 : Sydney, N.S.W.) - Buildings - Designs and plans. 3. Stadiums
- New South Wales - Sydney - Design and plans. 4. Sports facilities - New South
Wales - Sydney - Design and plans. 5. Sydney (N.S.W) - Buildings, structures, etc.
- Designs and plans. I. Title

725.82099441

Editor: Simon Blackall
Assistant Editor: Elly Bloom
Design: Kirk Palmer Design, Sydney
Printed and bound by South China Printing, Hong Kong
Colour separation: International Lithographic, Hong Kong

Publishers
Foreword

The publishers of this book are proud to be associated with a project of this magnitude, probably the largest in our nation's history. The new buildings required for Olympic events necessitated the collaboration of a considerable number of architects who had the vision to make this enterprise a success, and we wish to express our admiration for them. Fulsome praise is also due to the engineers and construction companies, suppliers and individuals whose joint efforts brought this huge project to fruition.

This is only the second time that the Olympic Games have been held in the Southern Hemisphere. When Sydney won the bid to host the 2000 Olympics it was cause for great elation.

Since then an enormous amount of planning has been undertaken, both for the construction of specific sporting stadia and also for the development of the necessary infrastructure to service the event. This in turn re-focused people's perception of Sydney from harbourside city to urban megalopolis. Almost by coincidence, the Olympic site at Homebush Bay is the geographical centre of greater Sydney and is fast becoming an alternative attraction to the beaches and city centre.

In tracing the development of the construction, this book records just why these Games have been described as the Green Olympics. The dedication to environmentally sustainable design with the employment of solar power, and the use of natural ventilation, cooling and lighting has been incorporated into the buildings at Homebush Bay. It is to be hoped that these initiatives will soon be incorporated into all building developments in Australia.

This book is a tribute to all those who participated in this great adventure.

Captions by Paul McGillick (all other text as credited)

OLYMPIA TO AUSTRALIA
Philip Goad

The history of the modern Olympic Games and its architecture is relatively brief, with twenty-three Olympiads held in twenty cities since Athens in 1896. This contrasts markedly with almost three hundred known Olympiads between 776BC and AD394, all held at Olympia, the birthplace of the Olympic Games in ancient Greece. The Olympics was a ritual festival, a celebration of the body held within a beautiful natural setting where one could commune with the gods spiritually and physically. Distant from Athens, Olympia gained its temples and its sporting buildings gradually: its Stadium (athletics); Gymnasium (training); Hippodrome (for chariot and horse-racing); Palestra (wrestling, boxing, jumping); Baths (swimming); and a Leonidaeum (gymnastics). It was a permanent sacred place but with an intermittent use. As spaces of physical contest, many of the ancient sporting structures have endured and developed as fundamental building types. Today, as types, they continue to inspire architects intent on perfecting the classical model.

The modern Olympic Games have brought many changes, with new sports requiring more sophisticated buildings. There are also new sporting landscapes, more spectators, more contestants and through television, the technological demands of an attentive global audience. With a crucial role as media backdrop, and as a demonstration of local design expertise, Olympic architecture has become a laboratory for innovation and excellence. Indeed, gold medals were awarded in 1924, 1928 and 1936 not just to athletes but also to buildings. Recently, several Olympiads have been the focus for combining daring engineering with provocative architecture, with seminal structures by Nervi in Rome, Tange in Tokyo, Otto + Behnisch in Munich, as well as Miralles and Pinos in Barcelona. The formalist heroism of these buildings has tended to overshadow other, perhaps more modest, but still significant architectural and urbanistic achievements within each of their respective cities.

In Sydney 2000, the architecture of Homebush Bay and its outlying sites echoes the vision of French educationalist and humanist Baron Pierre de Coubertin, the instigator in 1894 of the modern Olympic Games. From 1910, Coubertin called for a 'modern Olympia' – a place where all sports would be represented equally and democratically. As in the ancient Greek model and in Coubertin's 'modern' Olympia, each structure in Sydney has an equal part to play. Each is a participant in an entire ensemble. No one building dominates, and there is no single heroic piece. A carefully orchestrated series of lightweight steel structures, some very big, some very small, resonate against a delicate Australian landscape and the vast and intense light of the southern sky.

OLYMPIC CITY

Olympia may have been a permanent site but it was never a city. In the modern Olympics, the notion of a permanent home for the games was rejected in favour of sharing the event internationally – it was a symbol of global co-operation. A city would compete for the right to host the games. As a result, the roving nature of the Olympic Games has also meant a roving urban project, providing an opportunity to rethink the city. The infrastructure of the city can be expanded and local architects given a unique chance to exhibit their work to the world. The earliest games such as those at Paris (1900) and St Louis (1904) had no available stadia and had to make use of parks, university playing fields and construct numerous temporary buildings. Since 1908, when London constructed White City, the first modern Olympic stadium, every city has strived wherever possible to remake itself, to re-present itself to the world. For 1992, Barcelona used the Olympics as a project for its 'reconstruction'. Barcelona was to be traversed, a necessity due to the deliberate dispersion of sports and accommodation precincts. The whole city of Barcelona transformed into an 'Olympic mecca', Coubertin's definition of an almost totally urban Olympic site. By contrast, Sydney 2000 fits Coubertin's other model – 'modern Olympia' as a sports park, a self-contained precinct where spectators and contestants could live and walk to all events and facilities. The sheer concentration of sports venues, support buildings and the athletes' village in the one precinct make Sydney's satellite city of sport at Homebush Bay comparable to the planned urban intensity of only two other previous Olympic hosts, Mexico City (1968) and Munich (1972).

OLYMPIC THEATRE

Since the modern inception of the Games, a shift has occurred in the manner in which we perceive the Olympics. The Games have now become a spectator sport of global proportions, a media event linked to immense capital, political and aesthetic investment. As a result, every new sports structure must be designed not merely as a place for competition but also as a theatre, as a giant international studio, a backdrop to be seen by billions of

spectators around the world. This has meant new and increasing demands: the perfection of sightlines; the need for floodlights, electronic and digital scoreboards and video screens; corporate boxes and ever more sophisticated systems for hearing, watching, and recording each contestant's every move. Today's stadium architecture has transcended Olympia's classical heritage as freely disposed public spaces in the landscape. These sporting structures have to cater not just for immediate spectators but they must also provide acoustic ambience for a greater global grandstand. The athlete is not just a competitor but a performer. For millions of people, each Olympic Games will be remembered by an athlete in a particular space recorded on film or by photograph. The Opening and Closing Ceremonies become gala events and the architecture becomes the framework for spectacle.

OLYMPIAN ENTERPRISE

From the very beginning, the staging of a modern Olympic Games has represented a contradictory mix of genuine international friendship and unequalled generosity combined with national pride. Some of the earliest games, those at Paris (1900), St. Louis (1904), and London (1908) needed accompanying world trade expositions to make their staging possible. There are the limits of time and budget and no city wishes to fail economically. The decision in Sydney to pursue a strategy of design and construct consortiums, was a considered political, economic and aesthetic strategy. It has meant design consistency within a locally shared tectonic and material palette. It has meant the establishment of a new cultural and recreational centre in Sydney's western suburbs – a secondary pole to the landmark features of Sydney's downtown, its harbour and Opera House. It has meant that the Olympic Village was privately developed for resale after the Games. It has also meant the emergence of an Olympic Co-ordination Authority (OCA) which has divided up the commissions, knitted the entire process and eventual urbanism of Homebush Bay and each of the outlying sites into a unified whole. It has been an undertaking of Olympian proportions and one that will have a lasting effect on the people and city of Sydney.

OLYMPIC RIGOUR

In ancient Olympia, the language of architecture was the universal grammar of classicism. A picturesque collection of temples, colonnades and monumental statuary combined with steps, embankments and terraces. Graceful architectural consistency merged with a gentle manipulation of an already idyllic park-like landscape. In the modern Olympic Games, classical allusion was not always so subtle. Los Angeles had its arcaded Colosseum (1932), while in Berlin (1936), its similar scaled stadium suggested the imperial values of Ancient Rome. Other cities used their Olympiads to promote International Modernism as the century's new 'democratic' classicism and as a symbol of their own progressive cultures. Stadia at Amsterdam (1928) by Jan Wils, and Helsinki (1952, designed in 1940) by H. Lindegren were brilliant examples of the new International Style. Postwar Olympiads were the scenes of much bolder attempts at defining a new grammar of sporting structures. In the hands of Pier Luigi Nervi (Rome, 1960), Kenzo Tange (Tokyo, 1964), and Felix Candela (Mexico City, 1968), reinforced concrete became the means to new and expressive forms of stadium architecture. In Munich (1972), technological developments went even further. The visual armature for the main stadia, designed by Frei Otto and Gunter Behnisch, was a floating amorphous skin of translucent plexiglass suspended by steel masts.

In Sydney, the common language is that of the repetitive architectural section. It has been used in two ways: either to enclose or embrace the shape of the sports field it serves; or as an extrusion, a linear series with a view to infinite extension. Frames used in series, lines of trusses, marching rows of beams angled into the sky – the rigour is one of repetition. Driven by ecological sustainability, almost all of these sections are of composite construction and many use recycled timbers. Lightweight steel construction dominates and the result is a silhouette of spidery steel trusses, with an endless roof plane floating above the landscape. This structural consistency creates a fragile almost non-demonstrative aesthetic that in the open landscape of Homebush evokes the humility of a universal language of classicism.

AUSTRAL OLYMPIA

In Coubertin's plans for 'modern Olympia', he called for a building silhouette and a landscape that would be on equal terms; that would be harmonious:

'Terraces, flights of steps, embankments and inclined planes – these, we do not hesitate to say, would be one of the most certain sources of eurythmy for the Olympic city – and a guarantee of ample beauty and majestic grandeur for the ceremonies which would take place there.'

It is this notion of harmonious proportion between man-made structures and the natural environment that has been sought by only a very few Olympic cities. The link with nature was attempted in Mexico City (1968) with rock studded earth berms and inland Aztec-inspired mosaic murals. Stadia became organic components of an existing landscape. In Munich (1972), floating skin roofs became clouds above artificially contoured mounds enclosing seating and stadia. In Sydney 2000 the entire site at Homebush Bay is a remediated industrial and river estuary landscape. Buildings and surrounding parklands have been designed with the aim of a reconciliation and recuperation of the landscape. This has been achieved through a complete understanding of the inter-relationship of ecological issues affecting building and the environment. Eurythmy has been sought in the creation of this new Olympic site.

Ancient Olympia also had its own cultural component. At its centre there was a sacred grove dedicated to Zeus and the surrounding site combined athletic and cultural edifices. Paintings, sculptures and other works of art scattered the landscape. At Homebush, there is a fig grove, also at the site's centre, and a series of commissioned art works scattered across the site. At Olympia, olive trees were brought from Istria to plant the treeless and shadeless festival grounds. At Homebush Bay, the boulevard has been lined with trees and lighting pylons. There are fountains, steps and terraces inlaid with the names of previous Olympic Gold Medallists. Sydney 2000 at Homebush Bay and its outlying sites at Penrith, Bankstown, Blacktown and the water of Sydney Harbour constitutes a fitting return to original Olympic ideals.

A HISTORY OF PUBLIC ARCHITECTURE IN SYDNEY

Patrick Bingham-Hall

The two hundred years of settlement since the arrival of the First Fleet in 1788 have seen Sydney grow from an overgrown campsite to a city of nearly four million people. This evolution from penal colony to international city is reflected in its architecture and artistic history. Of particular interest, culminating in the massive program of design and construction for Sydney 2000, is the history of the city's public art and architecture. This history reflects the economic and technological growth of a dynamic city and features the spectacular architectural and artistic possibilities provided by such a uniquely beautiful place.

The earliest sporting events in colonial Sydney were held in paddocks and cleared land, with cricket and horse racing the pastime of choice for officers and settlers with money. An etching by Thomas Harvey Lewis (left), son of the Colonial Architect Mortimer Lewis, shows cricket being played in Hyde Park in 1841. An early race course was laid out at Homebush Bay in 1840, and Randwick racecourse was established in 1859. As the population grew rapidly after the discovery of gold, more formal structures were required for mass participation in public activity. The short-lived Garden Palace in the Botanic Gardens was the first grand realization of this, while temporary triumphal decorations were erected for royal visits and parades.

The first specific sporting venues in the early 20th century were built in the Moore Park precinct, with the Sydney Cricket Ground and a collection of halls and pavilions which were to become the RAS Showground. The Sydney Cricket Ground had individual grandstands in the Edwardian style, with the infamous 'Hill' being a large banked area for standing spectators. The models for the Sydney Cricket Ground and other suburban ovals were English county cricket grounds such as Lords and Old Trafford. This led to the incongruous sight of Rugby football games being played on a rectangular pitch within a circular field. During this period huge crowds attended events such as the GPS Head of the River regatta, and the cricket test matches against England.

HYDE PARK, 1841
(Watercolour reproduction
courtesy Mitchell Library)

Centennial Park was laid out on the swamps adjacent to Moore Park, and was a beguiling mixture of Australian landscape and inherited English sensibilities – as if Capability Brown had gone bush. This park established a continuing trend of revitalizing swamps and wasteland, and is a great urban park in the manner of Munich's Englischer Garten, the Bois de Boulogne in Paris, and New York's Central Park.

As Sydney is a city on the water and in the bush, the topography and the climate demand specific engineering and material requirements. Many vernacular decorative structures were built on the coast and the harbour foreshores as wharves and changing pavilions. A spectacular surviving example is Wylie's Baths, with spindly timber poles and decking clinging to the cliffs above Coogee Beach. Railways, trams and ferries were the main mode of transport, and Central Railway Station was Sydney's equivalent to Waterloo and the Gare du Nord. Its vaulted internal space, rather more humble than its European peers, is the natural precursor to the Olympic Park Railway Station at Homebush.

Hyde Park was redesigned in 1926 with an art-deco plan which had the vibrant Archibald Fountain as the nexus to the radiating paths of the northern half of park. The southern half was anchored by the

Photo courtesy of Mitchell Library

Photo courtesy of Mitchell Library

GARDEN PALACE 1879

Built in response to the growing popularity for international exhibitions, the Garden Palace was designed by Colonial Architect James Barnet, and completed in September 1879 in time to host the Colonial Exhibition. Set on a ridge on the eastern side of Macquarie Street with a floor area of 2.2. hectares topped by a 60 metre high dome, it overlooked Government House and Farm Cove. It was destroyed by fire in on 22 September, 1882.

This 220 hectare combination of cultivated
and wild parkland in the middle of
Sydney's eastern suburbs was dedicated
'to the enjoyment of the people of New
South Wales forever' on 26 January, 1888,
the centenary of the foundation of the
colony. On 1 January, 1901 it was the site
for establishing the Commonwealth of
Australia with the swearing in of the
nation's first ministry by the Governor-
General. Originally the source of Sydney's
water supply, the swamps are now home to
a rich variety of waterbird species.
Surrounding these lakes is an extensive
parkland including cultivated gardens,
picnic areas, horse riding trails, bicycle
tracks and playing fields.

Anzac War Memorial, one of Australia's most potent and moving monuments with bas-relief by Raynor Hoff and an heroic male nude sacrifice in the sanctum. The greatest manifestation of engineering on a grand scale was the Sydney Harbour Bridge, which captured both the glory of Sydney's geography and the Nietzchean symbolism of the between-war period.

The suburban spread and cultural restructuring of the fifties and early sixties saw little progress in the fields of public architecture and art. Sydney's legacy from this period is in the remarkable individual and inspirational private houses built by architects such as Harry Seidler, Sydney Ancher, Peter Muller, Neville Gruzman and Douglas Snelling. This architecture led to the recent well-known houses in suburban bushland by Glenn Murcutt, Ken Woolley, Rick Leplastrier and Peter Stutchbury.

The sixties brought expressive and elegant public sculpture, most famously the El Alamein fountain at Kings Cross. Similarly expressive and elegant was the network of concrete bridges built over Sydney's waterways. These bridges, taking their cue from those of Maillart in Switzerland and by Nervi between Florence and Bologna, create a wonderful thrust and counterbalance to the pervading greens, greys, and browns of the bushland and rivers they cross.

Expressive public buildings became synonymous with Sydney as a result of the Sydney Opera House. The original inspiration and genius, the ensuing conflicts and controversy, and the final resolution have given the residents of the city a building with which they identify in a unique way. This special relationship is also seen in Cairo with the Pyramids, Athens with the Parthenon, Florence with its Duomo, and in New York City with the Empire State Building.

A wave of confident and exuberant public architecture then swept through Sydney, leading up to the Bicentenary of white settlement in 1988. Philip Cox established a typology of white painted steel and curvaceous forms at Darling Harbour and with the Sydney Football Stadium. Public venues and facilities were now built as autonomous structures, rather than as a disparate collection of grandstands or pavilions. Public art also gained momentum after the completion of the Opera House with sculpture and installation work being actively encouraged and financed. The Edge of the Trees installation on the site of the First Government House by Fiona Foley and Janet Laurence is accessible, provocative, and profoundly moving.

The development of public art and architecture in Sydney, accelerated by the Olympics, reflects the romantic topography of the region and the transformation of a small colonial outpost into one of the world's most significant cities. Every large public building, every rejuvenation of public space and parkland, and every public art installation draws on the cultural and architectural heritage of the Sydney area. Simultaneously, they must now satisfy an increasingly knowledgeable and expectant public which anticipates nothing less than the best in the world.

CENTRAL RAILWAY STATION 1904 - 1908
Designed by Walter Liberty Vernon, Central Railway
Station remains a focus for the city, being the terminal
for interstate and country trains and the main interconnecting station for suburban trains. Neo-classical in
conception, its piers and viaducts (left) reflect the
characteristic use of sandstone in Sydney's institutional
and domestic architecture. The internal concourse
(above) with its vaulted ceiling and glass skylight
supported by steel trusses, is one of the few remaining
examples in Australia of the iron and glass construction
techniques which flourished in the 19th century.

ARCHIBALD FOUNTAIN 1932

The publisher, Jules François Archibald, left a bequest to provide a 'beautiful bronze symbolical open air memorial (above) by a French artist' to commemorate the friendship between Australia and France during World War I. François Sicard's group of bronze statues above a cluster of water-filled basins was presented to the City of Sydney on 14 March, 1932. It depicts Apollo as a symbol of beauty and light against a sunburst of water jets presiding over the figures of Diana, Pan and Theseus representing purity, plenty and civilisation.

ANZAC MEMORIAL 1934

Dominating Hyde Park South, the ANZAC Memorial (right) embodies the significance of World War I in Australia's coming-of-age. Dedicated in December 1934, its architect C. Bruce Dellit saw the Memorial not as a glorification of war, but as an acknowledgement of the qualities of courage, endurance and sacrifice which war occasions. It is a tall, domed hall mixing neo-classical and art deco styles. The internal circular Hall of Memory (opposite page) is illuminated by high, arched and glazed amber windows and centres on Rayner Hoff's sculptural tableau featuring a sacrificial soldier borne aloft on his shield and sword.

Photo (1954) courtesy of Mitchell Library

WYLIE'S BATHS 1907

Tidal baths are a feature of Sydney's water-focused culture. Wylie's Baths (above) are the most spectacular with timber sun decks articulated from the cliff above the pool and looking out to the Pacific Ocean. Allen Jack + Cottier's 1993 restoration kept the character of the baths even though most of the timber had to be replaced.

RAS SHOWGROUNDS, MOORE PARK

A collection of pavilions, stables, exhibiton halls and a large elliptical showring linked by a network of alleys and winding paths (left). Disparate architectural features such as Dutch-style gabled facades and massive Moderne internal exhibition spaces, make for an interesting heterogenous assemblage of buildings and precincts.

SYDNEY HARBOUR BRIDGE 1932

Construction of the Sydney Harbour Bridge (opposite page) commenced in 1929 with a design by the New South Wales Government Chief Engineer, J J C Bradfield. By the time it was opened to the public on 19 March, 1932 it had already achieved iconic status. It not only unified the two sides of the Harbour, but brought together art and engineering in a powerful symbol of the optimism of a still young country.

GREAT BRITAIN v. AUSTRALIA
Sydney Cricket Ground, July 19th 1958.
3rd and Deciding Test, won by Great Britain 40 Pts.
Australia 17 Pts.
Attendance, 68,720. Gate Receipts, £29,548·15·0.
All Ticket Test.
Equals World Record Gate Receipts.

SYDNEY CRICKET GROUND
In 1851 the army received permission to use land behind
Victoria Barracks as a Soldiers Cricket Ground and Rifle
Range. By 1875 the NSW Cricket Association was using the
ground and in 1878 the first inter-colonial cricket match was
held between NSW and Victoria. By 1909 most of the original
stands (Old Bob, Sheridan, Brewongle, Ladies, and Members)
had been built (above) and in 1938 the M.A.Noble stand
replaced the Old Northern Stand for the Empire Games. Since
World War II most of the original stands have been replaced.
The Members and the Ladies stands survive and are
picturesque pavilions in the Edwardian style.

EL ALAMEIN FOUNTAIN 1961
Designed by Woodward and Taranto, this luminous dandelion
is in Fitzroy Gardens in the heart of Kings Cross. Celebrating
the Australian army's role in the Battle of El Alamein during
World War II, the fountain (left) now symbolises the
bohemian lifestyle of Kings Cross in the Swinging Sixties.

SYDNEY OPERA HOUSE 1973
A building of such individuality (opposite page) that it seems
to owe no debt to any architectural predecessors, was won in
competition by Danish architect Jørn Utzon. The architect
resigned from the project in 1966 and left Australia, never to
return. This followed pressure from a government which, in
the face of a blow-out in costs, had lost its nerve. Enormous
controversy followed and continues to this day. The building
(mainly the interior) was completed with substantial revisions
to Utzon's original plans.

ROSEVILLE BRIDGE 1966
Swooping dramatically across Middle Harbour in a grand extended curve, the Roseville Bridge (above) was designed by the NSW Department of Main Roads with advice on general proportioning by the architectural consultants Fowell, Mansfield and Maclurcan. It is 400 metres in length between abutments and is constructed on a horizontal curve of over 650 metres radius.

SYDNEY UNIVERSITY BOATSHED 1965
An endearing steel structure painted to look like wood, triangular in section, on a quiet backwater of the Lane Cove River. The Sydney University Boatshed (left) designed by Denis Rourke, demonstrates an unpretentious vernacular adaptation of prevailing modernist forms in the style of the now revered 'Sydney School' of architecture.

GLADESVILLE BRIDGE 1964
A soaring white double arch linking Gladesville and Drummoyne over the Parramatta River, the Gladesville Bridge (opposite page) was designed by the consulting engineers Maunsell and Partners. The contract was let to the builders, Stuart Brothers of Sydney, with Reed and Mallik from England as the engineering contractors. More than 600 metres in length between abutments, it has a clear span of over 300 metres and a distance of 40 metres between the underside of the arch and the high water mark.

EDGE OF THE TREES 1995

The Museum of Sydney not only occupies the site of the first Government House in Sydney, but actually incorporates elements of the foundations and artefacts found on the site. Janet Laurence and Fiona Foley created Edge of the Trees (opposite page top) in the Museum's forecourt. Consisting of 29 pillars of steel, glass, sandstone and wood, the artwork evokes the botanic, Aboriginal and colonial past of the site. This is achieved with inscriptions in the pillars and through the barely discernible Koori voices naming sites of Aboriginal occupation around Sydney.

SYDNEY EXHIBITION CENTRE 1988

As part of the Bicentennial celebrations in 1988, Darling Harbour, formerly a derelict railway and shipping goods area on the western edge of Sydney's CBD, was opened as a multi-purpose public precinct. The Sydney Exhibition Centre (opposite page bottom), designed by Philip Cox Richardson Taylor and Partners, refers to a long tradition of steel and glass exhibition buildings. The structural system reflects maritime imagery, in particular the upright mast system with its horizontal spreader arm.

FEDERATION PAVILION 1988

This building resulted from a competition to replace the original Federation Pavilion in Centennial Park (1901). It was won by architect Alex Tzannes in 1986, with a quirky, slightly illogical neo-classical design. Circular in plan, it is topped by a floating copper-clad cupola (top left). Inside, the domed ceiling (left) is painted in a rainbow mosaic by artist Imants Tillers with typically ironic inscribed texts.

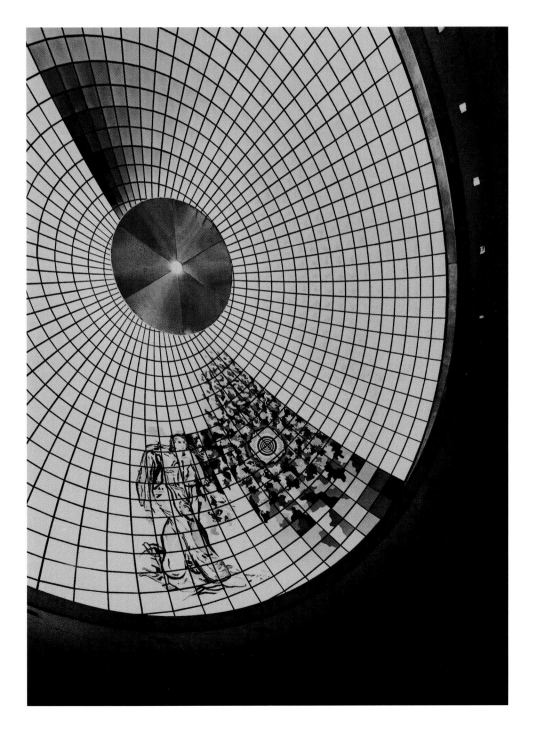

PLANNING THE OLYMPIC SITE
Chris Johnson

Planning the Olympic facilities at Homebush Bay was a complex task that built upon layers of history while presenting a confident statement about the future. The massive movement of hundreds of thousands of people to, from and between the various sporting venues had to be planned to perfection. But this huge sports complex is more than just a logistical solution for the two weeks of the Games. It is a long term legacy for the people of Sydney, and will celebrate local characteristics and skills in planning and designing the buildings and public spaces.

The site beside the Parramatta River on the upper reaches of Sydney's famous harbour has been waiting for significant use from the days of settlement. It has always been between two worlds; between the coast and the mountains, the sea and the forest. Even the early Aboriginal inhabitants saw it as a place between the Eora coastal people and the Dharug forest people. Four of the trees on the site had scar marks which may have indicated the direction for the Dharug people to head towards the coast.

So the place between two worlds began as a buffer zone. The Parramatta River flows across the site from the west to the much wider Sydney Harbour in the east.

THE EARLY ESTATES

Homebush has many significant connections to the quests of early European explorers in discovering the interior of their new land. A problem they confronted was how to cross the mountain range which separated the coastal strip from the inland. It was not until 1813 that the explorers Blaxland, Wentworth and Lawson crossed the mountains by following the ridges rather than the valleys. The Homebush connection is that relatives of two of the explorers, Blaxland and Wentworth, established the first large estates on the site.

John Blaxland, one of the first free settlers to arrive in Australia, acquired 520 hectares of land which he named Newington after his family estate in Kent. Blaxland established salt pans on the edge of the Parramatta River, from which he sent salt to Sydney each week. Newington House was built in 1832 and still stands today as part of the Silverwater Correction Complex. John's brother Gregory joined with William Charles Wentworth, the son of the owner of the adjoining estate, in the famous journey across the Blue Mountains.

D'Arcy Wentworth acquired 370 hectares of land between Powells Creek and Haslams Creek in 1810. He named the property 'Homebush' and started Australia's first horse stud there. In 1840 his son, William Charles Wentworth, built a new race course on the estate and was elected President of the Sydney Turf Club. The course was the headquarters of Australian racing until 1859 when Randwick was established. From very early days the Homebush site has been associated with sport and with oval-shaped venues surrounded by spectators.

ARMAMENTS AND ABATTOIRS

Unlike many of the early estates in Sydney, Homebush and Newington were not sub-divided into smaller housing lots. Newington was purchased by the Government in 1882 to become an armaments depot. In 1907, much of the Homebush Estate was resumed for the establishment of the State Abattoir. The Newington Estate, as the armament depot, had the advantage of conserving a large area of bushland and river edge. While a number of bunkers for the storage of ammunition existed on the site, these were spread out and some have now been incorporated into the Olympic Village. The rest of the site will become part of Millennium Parklands in the Year 2000.

The State Abattoir established a new pattern across the landscape that has had a direct influence on the planning of the Olympic facilities. At its peak, the abattoir employed 1600 people. The Administration Building, designed by Walter Liberty Vernon (an early Government Architect), has been restored and is now used as an information centre, and the grid of fences has left its impact on the Olympic Masterplan.

Homebush Estate built by D'Arcy Wentworth (above left). Wentworth acquired 370 hectares of land alongside Haslams Creek in 1810. His son William Charles Wentworth built a new racecourse on the Homebush Estate in 1840 adjacent to Parramatta Road.

View of the racecourse (above centre) at Homebush in 1854. The site has been a place of sport from the early days of settlement.

Newington House (opposite page and above right) built in 1832 by John Blaxland as the family home overlooking the Parramatta River. The building still stands today within the Silverwater Correctional Complex.

The State Abattoir at Homebush (left) employed 1600 people at its peak and is reputed to have been the second largest in the world. The pattern of the fencing system of the State Abbatoir holding yards (below), has been incorporated into the new masterplan.

The State Brickworks (above, top right) were established at the head of the bay in 1911. The gigantic brickpit from which the clay was extracted had a major impact on the landscape.

The site was divided into regular shaped paddocks with large fig trees to provide shade for the animals. This pattern of fencing has been incorporated into the new masterplan, and a row of palm trees to the north of the Administration Building has been retained. Many of the fig trees have been relocated to provide much needed shade for the Olympic spectators. The massive buildings of the abattoirs gave a hint of the size of buildings to come, as do the State Brickworks, established at the head of the bay in 1911. While the brickworks stopped and started over the years, they created major changes to the Homebush site. The gigantic brickpit from which the clay was extracted, was used as the location for the film 'Mad Max, Beyond Thunderdome'. It has now become the adopted home of the Green and Golden Bell Frog - an endangered species. Continuing the shaping of the landscape at Homebush during the 1950s, the Government undertook major land reclamations and landfills around the bays by dredging the Parramatta River. In the 60s and 70s the site became a dumping ground for much of Sydney's household and industrial waste. Both the abattoirs and the brickworks closed in 1988.

LOOKING FOR A NEW USE

By the end of the 1980s, the site was looking for new uses. With the closure of the abattoir and the brickworks the area carried a legacy of pollution and industrial waste. Situated in the geographic heart of Sydney, it needed a project of a grand scale that was big enough to remediate the site. In 1988 Bicentennial Park had been developed and the concept of a regional recreation facility was emerging. Another factor that contributed to the eventual solution was the proposal to relocate the Showground with the Royal Agricultural Society from Moore Park. The Moore Park site, which had been used by the RAS to bring the country to the city each Easter, was now to be converted into film studios and relocation to Homebush Bay was the preferred option.

Sydney had shown initial interest with the Olympic bidding process for the 1996 games, but the serious bid was for the 2000 Games. To demonstrate the strength of the bid, the Government began the design and construction of the Aquatic Centre and the Athletic Centre at Homebush, both designed by Philip Cox in conjunction with Peddle Thorp. These buildings were constructed on part of the Australia Centre, an industrial estate, and their location was to become a major influence on the eventual masterplan at Homebush.

THE OLYMPIC BID

Along with the construction of the two sports facilities at Homebush, a major design process began to plan facilities required for an Olympic Games. A competition was held for a design for the Olympic Village which was won by a group of younger architects that included involvement by Greenpeace. The Greenpeace proposal was jointly masterminded by

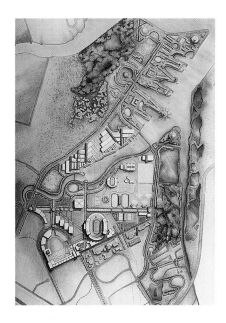

architect Rod Simpson and environmentalist Carla Bell, and the Green Agenda captured the imagination and the spirit of the bid. While the ideas for the village competition did not become the final scheme, much of the environmental and urban consolidation principles that were involved carried through.

The bid document did include a masterplan for the site, but it was prepared in a somewhat diagrammatic manner. Further masterplan options were developed by a team led by Philip Cox and included a scheme whereby the brickpit would be flooded in an attempt to make water a key feature of the site. Another competition at the time of the bid was for the Velodrome and this scheme has now been realised, although on a different site.

With Sydney winning the bid to host the 2000 Olympics, the planning became urgent and serious. A number of Government bodies were set up to co-ordinate activities, and a major design workshop was held to generate ideas. Some exciting design ideas were produced including a proposal by French architect Jean Nouvel, but the schemes were never released to the public. Much of this activity did not lead to direct results, but a change of State Government in March 1996 established a new single authority to plan and construct the Olympic facilities.

A 1988 perspective of the bid for the 1996 Olympics looking across a flooded brickpit to the Olympic Village with the sporting facilities behind.

THE OLYMPIC CO-ORDINATION AUTHORITY

The Olympic Co-ordination Authority was established in 1996 under David Richmond, and continued the work of a small masterplanning group led by Lawrence Nield to produce an overall masterplan for Homebush.

This masterplan established an urban core surrounded by Millennium Parklands. In the urban core, the orthogonal grid of the abattoir fields carried across the site to be sliced through by a new Olympic Boulevard. The Boulevard had to fit between the Australia Centre and the now constructed Aquatic Centre. The plan called for two types of buildings – object buildings and street edged buildings. The object buildings were clearly the stadia with the rest of the buildings designed to reinforce the street edge. The analogy was that of a city.

On the basis of this plan, the major buildings were allocated through a tender process either to contractors or to designers. Where the State was funding facilities, such as the showground replacement buildings or the railway station, the process was initially to select architects. Where the private sector was to fund all, or part of the facilities such as the stadium, or the village, the selection process was for finance, building and architectural design.

As the project began to evolve, some criticism was levelled at selection processes and at the apparent lack of design control. In response, the Director General of the OCA, David Richmond established a Design Review Panel under the Government Architect with wide ranging responsibilities to get the best design solution. While this led to quality design solutions for individual buildings, a growing concern developed about the spaces between

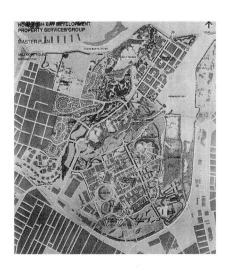

A Masterplan for Homebush Bay produced by MSJ Keys Young in September 1990. A number of options were produced ranging from minimal sports facilities to ones that included facilities for major international games.

A 1991 plan, produced during the bid process for the 2000 Olympics, showing an option which included the brickpit being filled with water. The plan was developed by a team headed by Philip Cox.

Perspective view of the bid proposal for the 2000 Olympics dated October 1992. This image was unveiled in Monte Carlo as part of the Sydney bid presentation.

The 1996 Masterplan produced by a group led by Lawrence Nield to pull together previous proposals from the bid documents into a Co-ordinated Masterplan for the whole site at Homebush Bay.

The revised Master Concept Design (right) developed at the end of 1996 by George Hargreaves with the Government Architect's Design Directorate and OCA. This plan put a new focus on the public domain at Homebush Bay.

the buildings - the public domain. The masterplan was again tested by those returning from the Atlanta Olympics where mass movement of people focused everyone's attention on the need for an adequate public domain at Homebush. A new masterplan that gave more attention to the public domain was clearly required and a major design workshop was established at the end of 1996 to achieve this.

PUBLIC DOMAIN MASTER CONCEPT DESIGN

The workshop concentrated on the creative input of an internationally acknowledged landscape architect, George Hargreaves. The decision to bring in an outsider was a complex one, but with construction happening at a great pace, it was essential to have a very strong advocate for the public realm and one who understood the problems of sites that needed remediation.

The final masterplan came about in a spirit of some urgency. It acknowledged the layers of history and the key planning concepts to date. It did, however, give the public domain an equal importance with individual buildings. In retrospect, the final design almost had to happen this way. It was an incremental planning approach starting with the gigantic individual buildings, followed by an intensive rethinking after Atlanta, which resulted in design modifications and improvements to co-ordinate the whole site. With time a critical factor, the new plan had to be implemented instantly. and it is amazing that so much of the initial design concept has carried through to the final solution.

The concepts of a large gathering space, with a park as a respite, the use of water, fig trees, public art and of quality street furniture have all been achieved. It is worth considering the structure and concepts behind the public domain master concept design. The plan is best described as being the combination of three moves: the red move to establish a paved centre on the site, the green move to connect landscape with the surrounding parklands and the blue move to celebrate water on the site.

THE RED LAYER

After seeing the large crowds at Atlanta it was apparent to those involved in planning the Sydney Games that space was a critical issue. The creation of a major Olympic Plaza as a central space at the Homebush site was a key design initiative. The plaza is capable of taking 300 000, but must also feel comfortable when only a few people are walking through. With buildings alongside that are the equivalent of 16 to 18 storeys high, their super scale needed a public place that was compatible. Space was deliberately left open at each end to connect with the landscape. The plaza began at the high point on the site and ended adjacent to Haslams Creek. The Olympic Boulevard became part of this space at its northern end but remained a tree lined avenue at the southern end. The plaza form was

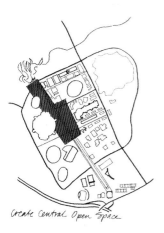

Create Central Open Space

emphasised by having trees located only on its edges. To provide shade, human scale and lighting, a series of pylons was placed across the plaza – 13 metres high to reflect the heroic scale. The solar collectors which power the lighting on these pylons act as a verandah to the public space.

The large object buildings of Stadium Australia and the SuperDome engage the plaza rather than complete it. The edges are loosely defined by an urban forest of trees that provide shade and a less formal atmosphere around the two large sports buildings.

The large open space is where most people arrive by train or by bus. The railway station deposits 30 000 people an hour onto the plaza, while bus stations at each end lead people to and from the suburbs of Sydney. At a detailed level, the pattern of the plaza responds to the original abattoir grid and the new boulevard angle set at 9°. A backgammon pattern is created with interlocking paving in earth colours - one ochre and one red. Symbolically, the earth is represented in colours that are very Australian. The lighting pylons continue the earth relationship, with solid concrete feet supporting lighter metal towers. These then respond to the language of lighting towers across the site.

THE GREEN LAYER

The design workshop concluded that the urban core was not likely to become a city. Homebush was more a place of events on a large scale and its connection with the surrounding landscape was therefore important. Fingers of green were planned to spread out from the boulevard and the plaza into Millennium Parklands. These were designed to be more formal on the north and become more informal as they moved towards the south. Each finger was therefore to have a different character.

The finger alongside the railway station is very graphic, with flowering jacaranda trees and Mongolian plums giving a delicate yet colourful route for pedestrians. Alongside this avenue of trees are the commercial facilities with the railway station a focus. Another response from seeing the Atlanta Olympics was the need for Homebush to incorporate more park-like spaces with green lawns and trees. The central park – 'the overflow', was originally planned for commercial development, but has now become landscaped into a fine park. This enabled the existing alley of mature trees such as eucalypts and brush boxes to be kept. At the southern end a change of level creates an amphitheatre for performances and a curved drainage channel from the abattoirs is retained and interpreted through public art. This is where Boundary Creek is located, a landscape of wetland trees, water gums and sheoaks reinforce the natural feel of the landscape. Artwork adds poetry to the site by placing floating wands in the water with drifting mist, so that viewers on the bridge above feel connections to nature and to water.

On the eastern side of Olympic Plaza a row of large trees gives shade and definition. An early idea was to use replanted trees from the site but there were insufficient numbers. In an

Engage Major Buildings

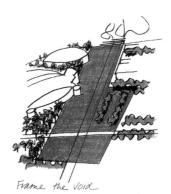

Frame the Void

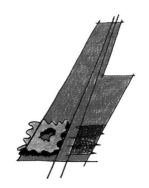

Emphasize High Point

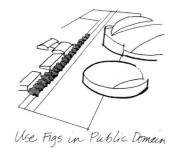

Use Figs in Public Domain

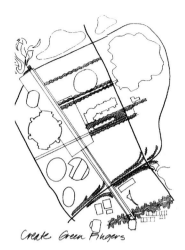

Create Green Fingers

Water at High and Low Points

Aerial View of the new Olympic Plaza which emerged during the Master Concept Design workshop with George Hargreaves and team.

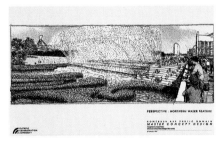

The northern water feature is the culmination of the new Olympic Plaza as well as a visual demonstration of the process of purifying and cleansing water collected on the site.

incredible piece of theatre, mature figs were shipped down from Tweed Heads, by barge, and towed under the Harbour Bridge to Homebush Bay.

THE BLUE LAYER

The universal image of Sydney is one of water, whether it is beaches or the harbour. Homebush is just off the harbour, with Haslams Creek and Boundary Creek weaving through the site on their way to the Harbour. The master concept plan places water at either end of the plaza. This emphasises the high point on the site as well as the two low points. The water feature to the north collects all surface water on that part of the site and cleanses it for reuse. This is done through ponds with cleansing plants as well as through aeration of the water by a giant fountain that casts water high into the air. From the plaza the fountain will be an exciting celebration of the site and of environmental systems.

Almost as a reference to the harbour the main pond has a jetty that allows visitors to engage in the water feature and to understand the water cleansing systems. An artwork by Ari Purhonen nestles under the jetty, using a rainbow of colours incrementally adjusting the nine degrees of difference within the site grids.

Water is also used at the southern end of the plaza with large ponds set amongst replanted fig trees. Fountains spray above pathways, enclosing visitors in a veil of water. Both features are of heroic scale and are deliberately designed in an abstract manner rather than copying nature. At the southern end, the visitor's relationship to water is less dramatic and is one of observation from three bridges above.

ENSURING DESIGN QUALITY

Having established a master plan to guide development the Design Review Panel, which included professors of architecture and landscape architecture as well as key figures from the arts and heritage communities, had to see it implemented.

Each project, building or public domain went through an exhaustive review process to ensure quality. This occurred from the largest buildings to the smallest elements including street lights, seats and garbage bins.

Signage was an important part of the process and the graphic quality of the site was vital to understanding its layout. The Design Review Panel became closely involved in selecting architects for certain projects. This was particularly so in encouraging architects from smaller practices to be able to undertake projects on the Olympic site. The Panel closely monitored the Olympic Village project to help achieve a balance between design excellence and commercial viability. One of the real legacies of the Olympics will be the spin off into the rest of the housing sector in New South Wales and the increasing use of Environmentally Sustainable Design (ESD) principles for most building types.

Planning is certainly not a static process. The Homebush site has gone through many stages of evolution from the early estates of Wentworth and Blaxland to abattoirs and finally to Olympic planning. Buildings have come and gone from various master plans. Public transport has been refined from many options. The Public Domain has been given a great boost and the process of caring for detail has continually been stressed.

The end product is now an exciting venue, and a dynamic new urban environment - particularly appropriate for Sydney in the year 2000. The planning process set up opportunities for some of Australia's best designers to produce a lasting legacy for Sydney although Homebush will continue to change and be refined. Designing for the Olympics has set a benchmark that future planning will need to work hard to achieve. The final place, as so often happens with a green (or brown) field site, will only really be understood when its landscape has matured and layers of use, of decoration and of celebration have built up over the years.

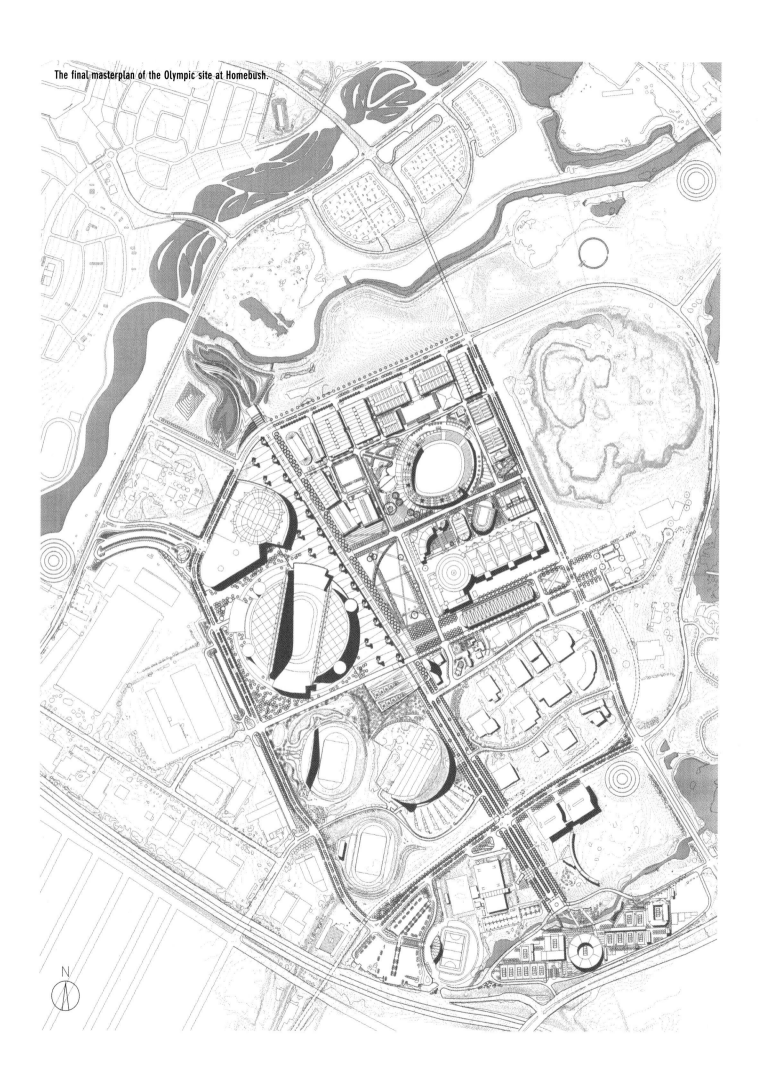

The final masterplan of the Olympic site at Homebush.

N

GREATER SYDNEY ▲

1   Sydney International Regatta Centre, Penrith Lakes
2   Sydney International Shooting Centre, Cecil Park
3   Duncan Gray Velodrome, Bankstown
4   Sydney International Equestrian Centre, Horsley Park
5   Sydney Exhibition Centre & Sydney Convention Centre, Darling Harbour
6   Sydney Football Stadium, Moore Park
7   Olympic Sailing Shore Base, Rushcutters Bay
8   Olympic Sporting Facilities, Aquilina Reserve, Blacktown
9   Ryde Aquatic Leisure Centre
10 Olympic Site, Homebush

HOMEBUSH ▶

1   Bicentennial Park
2   Millennium Parklands
3   The Brickpit
4   Stadium Australia
5   Lighting pylons
6   Olympic Park Railway Station
7   Sydney Showgrounds
8   Sydney Showgrounds Exhibition Halls
9   Sydney Showgrounds Showring/Baseball
10 Sydney Showgrounds Animal Pavilions
11 Homebush Bay Ferry Wharf
12 State Hockey Centre
13 Sydney International Athletics Centre
14 NSW Tennis Centre
15 Sydney International Aquatic Centre
16 Olympic Village
17 Sydney SuperDome
18 Homebush Bay Novotel Ibis Hotel
19 Sydney International Archery Park

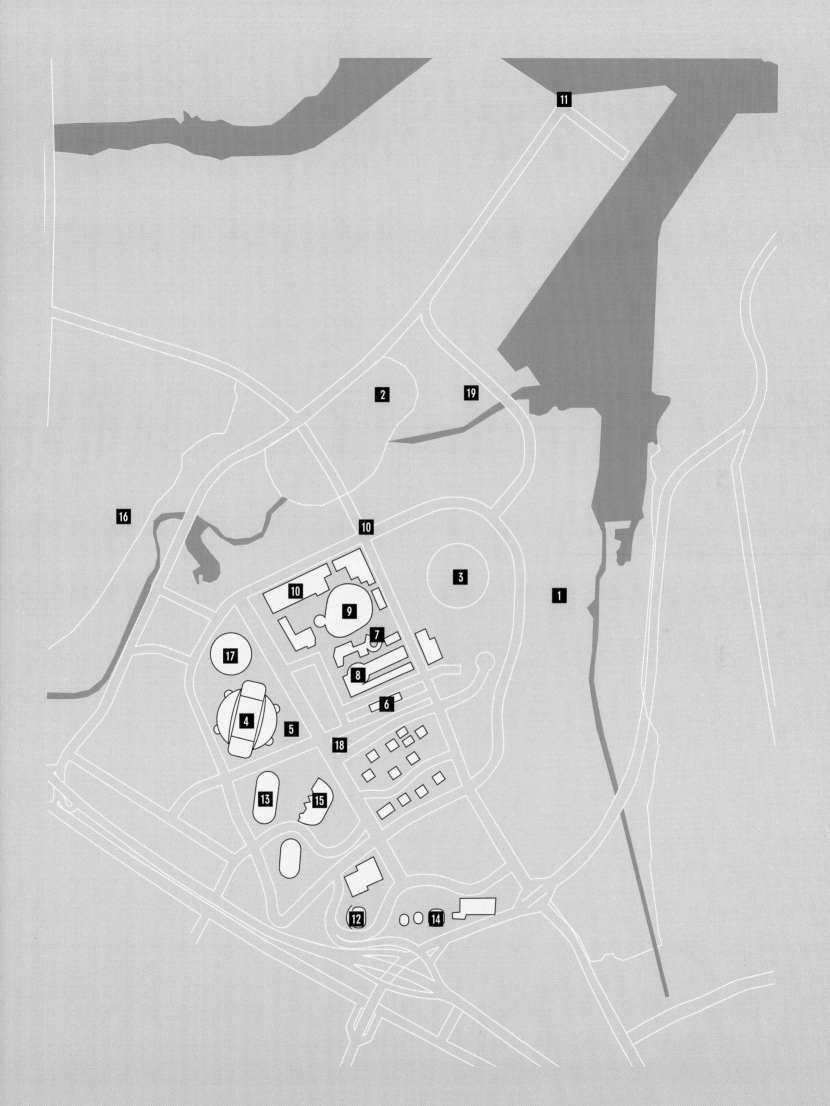

THE GREEN GAMES
Paul McGillick

C alling Sydney's Olympics the Green Games is more than an exercise in nick-names – the environmental guidelines for the Summer Games set out an ambitious strategy reflecting world-wide hopes for an ecologically saner new millennium.

Like so much of the Olympics effort, the Green Games will leave a valuable legacy, not just at the Olympics site, but throughout the greater Sydney area. This is because of a growing recognition that the Green Games initiatives can act as a model for the whole of Sydney. By following the Olympic Co-ordination Authority's 3R philosophy – Reduce, Re-use, Re-cycle – advocates say that Sydney has a ready-made strategy for confronting a looming environmental crisis. This involves water conservation, air and water pollution monitoring, conservation and regeneration of the natural environment, conservation of wildlife, a rational public transport infrastructure and accessible and adequate areas for public recreation.

REDUCING WASTE

Waste cannot be entirely avoided. However, its creation can be minimised. Of the waste which is generated, it is important also to lessen the amount dumped as landfill. One way to do this is through re-cycling.

During the construction on the Olympics site, re-cycled materials were used where possible. The most obvious example has been the re-use of rock and earth excavated for particular venues, then processed and moved to other sites – for example, in creating the landscaped embankments at the International Athletics Centre. Concrete and masonry rubble from the abattoir has been used elsewhere at Homebush Bay, while crusher dust has been re-used as pipe bedding and after-treatment in water quality control ponds.

The strategy of the Olympic Co-ordination Authority is to maximise the re-use of building materials, paper, cardboard, aluminium and glass waste created during the construction process. This process will continue after the Games, encouraged by a system of waste disposal bins and re-cycling facilities. In fact, the strategy itself will continue to evolve as guidelines are developed for the re-use of cups, plates and cutlery, together with the re-cycling of animal waste and bedding at the Showground.

Non-manufactured materials have also been included in the re-cycling process. Mulch produced by processing vegetation waste is used for plant beds to reduce water loss, while tree prunings are chipped and re-cycled. Stormwater is collected and used for dust-suppression and irrigation, while all animal and plant waste will be composted and used as fertiliser.

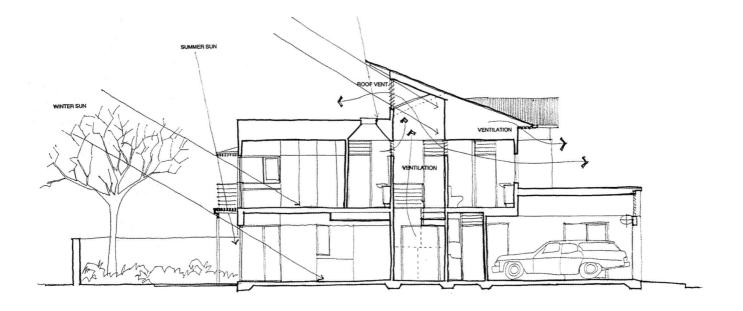

SAVING ENERGY

The aim here has been to minimise reliance on energy from non-renewable sources, exploit solar and wind power and maximise the efficiency of power use through energy-saving appliances.

For example, reliance on power-generated lighting has been reduced by orienting buildings to the sun and by the use of natural light through both windows and translucent ceilings. Optimal use of natural lighting, together with the use of motion-detectors for night-time lighting, are other ways in which the need for energy will be reduced.

The orientation of buildings is also a strategy for reducing the need for air-conditioning, either by taking advantage of southerly summer breezes or by devising systems of cross-ventilation – a strategy supported by the use of sunshields, light-coloured exterior finishes and wind-powered ventilators. In Stadium Australia itself, over-sized lift shafts, stairwells and escalator voids have been designed to draw in cooler air and allow warmer air to escape.

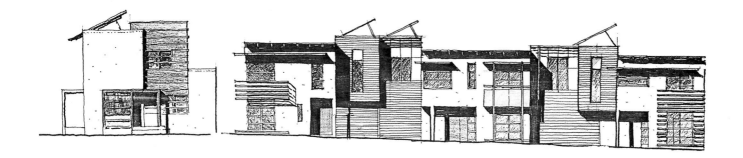

Perhaps the most significant component in the energy-saving strategy is the use of solar power. The Athletes' Village, for example, has solar panels fitted to the roof of every house. These panels provide energy for lighting and heating and assist the gas hot water systems. The use of solar power and natural gas is estimated to halve the greenhouse gas emissions which a village of this size would normally produce. The Village is the largest solar-powered suburb in the world, using about 75% less grid electricity than a suburb of comparable size.

Likewise, part of Stadium Australia's energy needs are met by solar power through two 500-kilowatt gas-fired co-generation engines, reducing greenhouse gas emissions by an estimated 40%.

WATER CONSERVATION

Water strategy at Homebush Bay has three aspects — water conservation, re-cycling, and quality controls on stormwater run-off into nearby waterways. The major aim is to make Homebush Bay as self-reliant as possible in its water needs. Drinking water will be supplied by Sydney Water, but most other water needs will be met by the use of stormwater and re-cycled water.

Stormwater will be treated in artifical wetlands, and sewage in the water reclamation plant. After treatment, the water will be used to flush toilets and irrigate landscaped areas. At the Showground, half of all water needs will be met by using rainwater stored in underground tanks and topped up when necessary with re-cycled water.

Before being discarded into local waterways, stormwater will be treated. This will be done through water quality control ponds that do the job normally done by naturally-occurring freshwater wetlands, reducing nutrients and sediments which would otherwise flow into Homebush Bay or the Parramatta River. The water quality control ponds will also be landscaped with native plants that naturally remove nutrients from stormwater run-off.

More efficient domestic appliances (dual-flushing toilets, efficient shower roses, drip irrigation devices), the use of roof-collected rainwater and appropriate landscaping and irrigation techniques will also contribute to the water conservation strategies of Homebush Bay. This will be augmented by planting mainly drought-resistant trees and the use of mulch to minimise evaporation. A computer-controlled irrigation system will provide automatic night operation and eliminate over-watering. It is estimated that water conservation and re-cycling initiatives will halve the water consumption of Homebush Bay.

THE PARKLANDS
Paul McGillick

By the time it is completed in 2010, the Millennium Parklands will be one of the world's largest urban parks. Given the environmental strategies driving the project, it will also be one of the world's greatest metropolitan parks. More than just a place for picnics, walking, cycling and horse-riding, Millennium Parklands will be an ecological observatory, re-connecting the citizens of a modern city state with a landscape restored to the pristine condition it enjoyed before white settlement.

About 420 hectares surrounding the Olympic site and Showgrounds will be completed in time for the Games. The remaining 450 hectares will be developed over the following ten years, linking the Parklands to existing recreational areas and providing many points of access.

BICENTENNIAL PARK

The Parklands include a mix of wetlands, woodland and grassland. A large part of this had been degraded by insensitive industrial use and its rehabilitation will be one of the great legacies left by the Games to the people of Sydney. Part of this rehabilitation was carried out as early as 1988 with the creation of Bicentennial Park which abuts the Olympic site.

The restoration of the mangrove wetlands was one of the great achievements of the Park and was part of the general rehabilitation of the Upper Parramatta River. Now the sea wall has been opened up to allow the tide to flush the salt marsh and mangroves, and fish and crabs have begun returning to the area. The mangroves provide a striking contrast to the open spaces of the upper park. Visitors access the mangroves by timber boardwalks, entering a zone of meditative calm and silence. Roots like primeval snorkels reach up out of the oxygen-starved mud to suck in air for the mangrove trees, and the visitor experiences a sense of continuity with an ancient past.

MILLENNIUM PARKLANDS

A part from the landscaping and public art, the Parklands are about conservation, regeneration and rehabilitation.

North Newington, for example, is an area north of the Athletes' Village. It is an invaluable ecological resource containing wetlands and rare woodlands. It is home to an estimated 160 species of birds, including some listed as endangered and at least ten species of migratory birds. Like the nearby Cumberland Plain, the area includes original forest with mature eucalypts. These forest areas, in turn, support the herbs, grasses and shrubs which provide a habitat for diverse birds, mammals and reptiles. Also included in this conservation area is built heritage, such as the Navy armaments building at Newington and the Homebush abattoir buildings which now function as a visitors' information centre. Protecting the natural conservation areas are buffer zones of local plants, separating them from development sites.

As well as conserving Homebush Bay's natural heritage, the Parklands strategy aims to regenerate those areas which have beem degraded by many years of pollution, land

reclamation and waste dumping. From the early 1800s, a complex estuarine system of forest, grasslands, waterways, salt marsh and mangrove wetlands was gradually lost. Now much of the industrial waste is being re-located as part of a pollution management plan which will result over time in a restoration of the natural life of the Bay and its environs. A water management strategy forms part of the regeneration program to reduce reliance on the water resources of greater Sydney. This involves utilising stormwater, roof water and re-cycled water from the Athletes' Village and Homebush Bay area for irrigation of the Parklands.

Haslams Creek winds its way gently through the middle of the Parklands down to Homebush Bay. Where the creek meanders south towards the Olympics site itself, some 55 000 cubic metres of waste was removed to a nearby landfill to create a 25 metre high mound covering 30 hectares. Gabion stone walls support the mound, now known as Kronos Hill, which offers splendid views over the entire Olympics site and Parklands. As part of the regeneration programme, 37 800 native trees and more than two million wallaby grass seedlings have been planted on the mound and down into the Haslams Creek valley.

THE BRICKPIT

Homebush Bay's chequered industrial past includes a saltworks, an abattoir, a naval armaments depot, waste dump and brickworks. Conservation of the area includes not just the natural heritage, but part of this industrial heritage as well. The brickpit, on the eastern edge of the Olympic site, has become a symbol of the way Homebush Bay has fused its natural and industrial history together. In fact, the huge, crater-like brickpit has taken on its own identity with its unique landforms, its ageing industrial buildings and the vegetation which has made its home there.

Also making its home there is the Golden Bell Frog, now very rare in Eastern Australia, with only twelve known breeding colonies in Sydney. A colony of some 300 has lived in the Brickpit for the last 20 years. Since the discovery of the colony in 1992, plans to develop the Brickpit have been put on hold, the only changes being a clean-up of the rim to create a horse trail and walking track. To further protect the frogs, additional habitats have been established and frog-proof fences erected to safeguard the frogs from crossing into dangerous roadways and construction sites.

The legacy of the Olympics will be a great parklands area for the citizens of Sydney, mixing a regenerated natural environment with discreet human interventions in the form of landscaping and site-specific art works. Most importantly, the strategy for the renewal of Homebush Bay has not stopped short at a landscape which is simply picturesque. Much of the parklands and wetlands have been left in their naturally rough and untidy state. Crucially, the human history of the area has been allowed to co-exist with its natural history, creating a valuable sense of connection between past and present – a sense of belonging in a city which has frequently ignored its natural and its built heritage.

Architect HOK Lobb in association with Bligh Voller Nield
Construction Multiplex and Obayashi
Engineering Modus Consulting Engineers and Sinclair Knight Merz

STADIUM AUSTRALIA

The centrepiece of this and every Olympics, the open-air stadium christened Stadium Australia, tops the enigmatic mark of 100 000 spectators and is the largest Olympic venue to date. In use from early 1999, the stadium is in fact a highly adaptable sporting arena. Conceived as a series of changing arrangements for athletes and spectators alike, the stadium is at its most impressive in Olympic mode. This is the grandest of its configurations, with the largest sporting area and the greatest crowd capacity. A year after the Olympics, its moment of greatest glory past, the two uncovered seating areas to the North and South will be largely dismantled, reducing the capacity from 110 000 to 80 000.

The stadium's viability rests on its life after the Olympics and Paralympics. The adjoining warm-up arena will become Sydney's premier athletics venue, and Stadium Australia will continue as the largest sporting venue in the city, accommodating a range of local passions. This is more complex than it might appear – there is no single dominant football code across the country, although in Sydney the two Rugby codes, League and Union, have the greatest following. Nonetheless the other great national code, Australian Rules, will also make use of the stadium. The expanse of an athletics track is unsuitable for football, where spectators demand a more intimate atmosphere with seating as close to the action as possible. To the North and South seats will be relocated to enclose the playing field. Below the major seating, East and West, the lowest level of seats will be moved forward. This tier will remain mobile, allowing the transformation of the stadium surface from a rectangular Rugby field to an oval Australian Rules or cricket venue in a matter of eight hours.

The effort and ingenuity expended in building such a high degree of flexibility into the structure has ensured that the stadium will maintain a high level of comfort and spectator involvement over its projected life span. It is a curious anomaly that Sydney had no large-capacity sporting venue to match the Melbourne Cricket Ground, which can accommodate upwards of 80 000 and can generate sporting events charged with true big-city excitement and spectacle. The range of sports followed in Sydney and their differing requirements has meant separate, smaller venues to date. Thus the largest legacy of the Olympics, Stadium Australia, will fill a void in the sporting life of a city which finds in its sports theatre, heroism, humour and even political comment.

Mindful of the demands of the city's own sporting public, the designers of Stadium Australia have extended the same level of comfort to Olympic spectators. The key elements of clear sightlines, as well as numerous amenities and easy access and egress have shaped the design. The low-slung polycarbonate roof shelters upwards of 60 000 spectators from

eddying showers whilst maintaining clear vision for the uppermost spectators in Olympic mode, when the sporting arena is at its widest. Four spiral ramps discharge the crowd to ground level fifteen abreast, with the open spaces surrounding the stadium allowing easy dispersal to the nearby train station, the carparks and buses and ferries.

The stadium was also partly funded through the sale of 30 year membership and corporate packages which give purchasers access to a wide range of events on the Stadium Australia sporting calendar. To cater for these users the western stand houses within its bulk a range of bars and dining areas. Together these constitute a large club, arranged on several levels around a deep atrium with scissoring escalators.

Sport in the new millennium will involve even vaster sums of money than is the case today. As entertainment, as spectacle, as drama, the sporting world demands of its venues that each important moment reverberates, first as a live event in front of as large a crowd as possible, then across countless homes with the growth of sports broadcasting, and thirdly as replays which stretch out the moment to be admired again. The desire for replays has now become part of the game itself, with players and spectators alike turning to the huge screens to relive the preceding event, with its glory and occasional injustice. Mindful of this, Stadium Australia has been configured to accommodate future digital technology where each seat has access to small screens providing both replays and a range of additional information.

The structure of the stadium also gives some clues about local building practices. In a country which experiences periodic shortages of skilled labour, building techniques have come to favour innovation and the widespread application of plant and specialised equipment. These conditions suit steel fabrication, where many of the components are manufactured off-site, and are then transported to the site and quickly erected and fixed in place. The sight of the two main arches supporting the stadium roof being hoisted aloft during construction provided a moment of engineering awe as their bulk was matched by that of the hoisting crane, the largest moveable one in Australia and amongst the largest in the world. The building is also mindful of resources where possible: rainwater falling on the roof is gathered and reused, and cooling systems using natural convection currents have been designed to vent the enclosed public areas.

Stadium Australia is representative of the world's major sporting facilities at the ticking over of the millennium. Located near the demographic centre of Sydney as it sprawls across the Cumberland Plain, the structure is large enough to accommodate the greatest of sporting spectacles, flexible to ensure its ongoing viability through continuous use, and mindful of the level of amenity and accessibility required to draw spectators out of the comfort of television viewing and into the moment when athletes and spectators are bonded, each driving the other, to create sport's sublime moments. HARRY MARGALIT

Plan: Olympic Mode

Plan: Post Olympic Mode

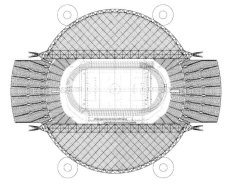

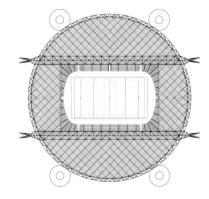

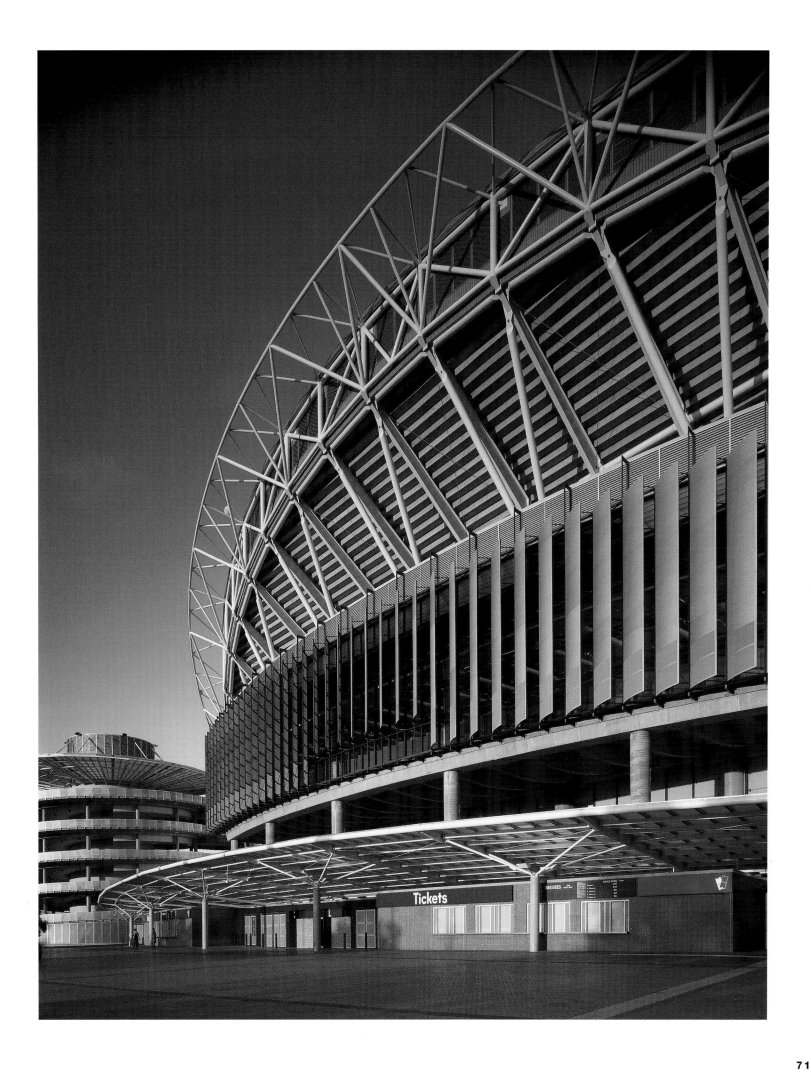

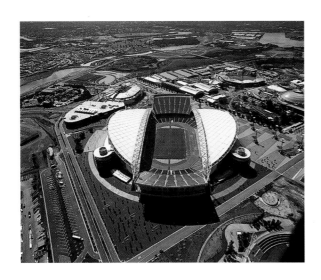

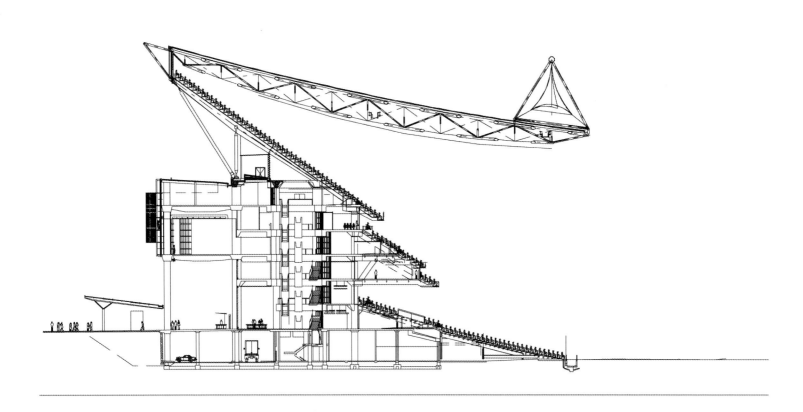

The east entrance faces Olympic Plaza and the railway station 600 metres away. Reaching a height equivalent to fourteen storeys, the stadium simultaneously expresses the dynamic spirit of the Olympic Games and the character of Sydney. The soaring curved trusses support roofs on the eastern and western sides, giving shelter to an estimated 60 000 spectators and offering a visual reference both to the Sydney Opera House and the Sydney Harbour Bridge. Four massive spiral ramps, each topped by a feisty circular parasol roof, are not only entry and exit points for large numbers of people, but also act as giant natural ventilation shafts. The circular ramps in turn relate to the circular plan of the stadium as a whole, hinting at the Olympic symbol of interlocking rings.

The construction of Stadium Australia was a spectacular process which provided an almost operatic sequence of changing vistas and dramatic set pieces. The heroic engineering and architectural visions were realised as the vast elongated arches and trusses built up a massive exoskeleton of white-painted steel, soon to be fleshed out and made football-friendly.

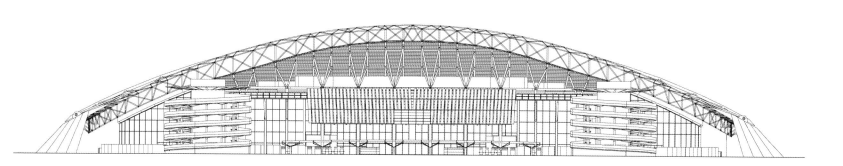

OLYMPIC PLAZA

Master Concept Design Hargreaves Associates/GADD

Construction Multiplex and Abigroup

Engineering Maunsell McIntyre

Project Management Gutteridge Haskins & Davey

PUBLIC DOMAIN

The dynamic vaulting roof and grand escalators of the railway station make for a dramatic arrival. As visitors step out on to the broadwalk and see the monumental structures on Olympic Plaza, their experience of this sporting complex is not simply that of spectators, but of participants. Important ingredients in this experience are the parklands and works of public art. Just as important are the various amenities, street furnishings, lighting pylons and signage which turn the spaces between the sporting and entertainment buildings into pleasant and stimulating moments of recreation. This is the public domain of Homebush Bay; human in scale, attractive in presentation and sensitive to the history and character of the site.

An intriguing opposition of past and present is established immediately by the restored brick and tiled buildings of the State Abattoir headquarters on the left of the railway station, now serving as the Visitors' Centre. The Overflow Park opposite the Stadium provides sanctuary with its original brushbox and eucalypt trees. Heading south along Olympic Boulevard is Fig Grove which features ten mature, re-planted Moreton Bay figs to complement the fountains and watercourse which play so subtly with the topography.

The Boulevard, which forms the spine of the Olympic complex, and the Plaza are necessarily huge, needing to accommodate up to 300 000 people a day. The 30 metre high pylons light this vast area and also help to offset the potential these spaces have for dwarfing human beings. Their scale also acts as an intermediary between street level and the soaring heights of the nearby stadia.

The light pylons are the first and perhaps most obvious signal to the visitor that the infrastructure of Homebush Bay is driven as much by design as it is by function. The result is a heightened quality of experience as the visitors make their way to and from venues.

Signage, bus shelters, public seating, re-cycling points and the backgammon-patterned red and ochre paving of the Plaza are all calculated to balance function with aesthetic sensitivity.

Even the amenities blocks defy convention, announcing themselves in a witty and flirtatious way. In fact, the buildings are strikingly original both in design and materials with their jaunty sail-like roofs clothed in a delicate teflon fabric, providing a light-filled interior as well as acting as a sign of their location.

Overall, the public domain has been designed to balance the grand scale of the Olympics and its venues by creating a more human, more connected and more relaxed experience at ground level. PAUL McGILLICK

The nine bus shelters at Homebush Bay have been designed as simple, elegant steel structures consisting of hollow section frames clad in aluminium sheets. The roofs are planar forms supported by rows of thin columns and the bays of glazing relate to the stainless steel seating.

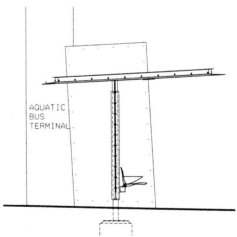

AQUATIC BUS TERMINAL

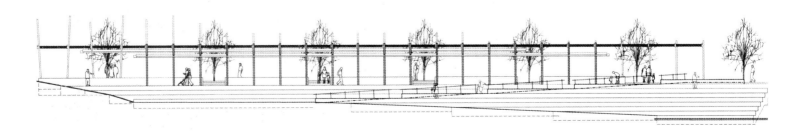

Taking its name from the Aboriginal word meaning meeting place, the Yulang functions as a respite point between the railway station and the stadium. It stands at the edge of the Plaza, connected on the west side by steps down to the Overflow Park. The aim was for a simple structure which did not look like a building, which was durable, resistant to graffiti and had a clean line. The result is a planar structure whose three roofs seem to float. Two roof planes, supported from the centre, are overlapping but not connected. The third is a colonnade structure with tension cables which will eventually be covered in vines.

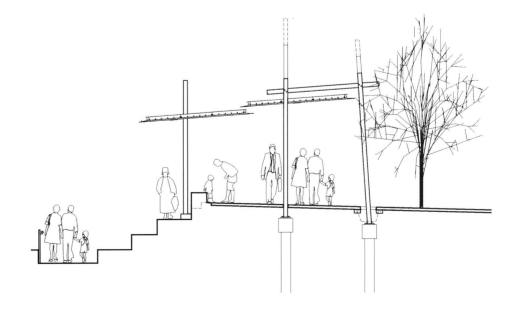

At the southern end of Olympic Boulevard, three bridges cross Boundary Creek to link the Tennis Centre with the rest of the Olympic site. The size, number and location of the bridges, tough symbols of Homebush's industrial past, were determined by crowd massing studies and anticipated crowd critical points. The bridges range in width from 3.5 to 7.5 metres and consist of steel on concrete pylons with blackbutt timber planking and sides clad in woven mesh with vertical rods running down the length of the trusses. Each bridge has a steel plate gangway at either end which acts as an intermediate element between land and bridge. Lighting on the trusses and gangways make the bridges glow at night.

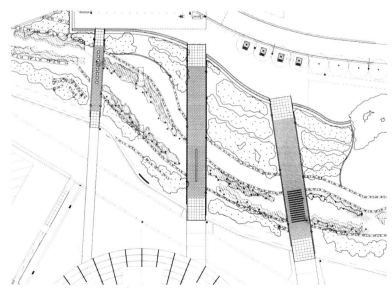

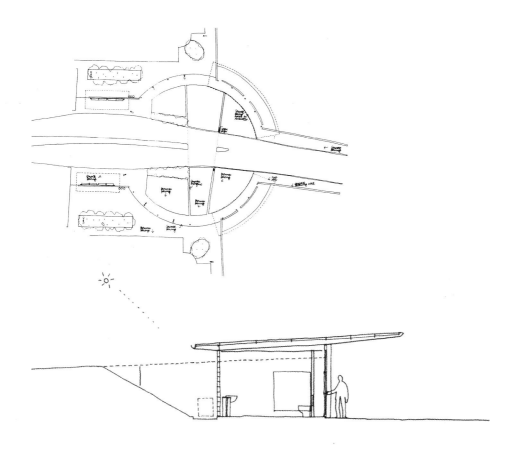

HILL ROAD CARPARK AMENITIES
Architect Ancher Mortlock & Woolley
Construction Lahey Constructions
Engineering Maunsell McIntyre
Project Management Gutteridge Haskins & Davey

The Hill Road Amenities Centre acts as a focus and orientation point between the Sydney Showgrounds and the Millennium Parklands carpark. It comprises toilets, kiosks, information, bus ticket machines and cashiers. A circular configuration of the civic space connects the Centre to the adjacent bus shelters. Set into earth mounds rising up from Haslams Creek, the two buildings are contained in tapered pre-cast concrete walls extending out into the landscape along the main pedestrian pathways. The Centre and the shelters are steel-framed structures with cantilevered aerofoil floating roofs that hover above the earth mounds, acting as a directional beacon for people returning to their cars.

NORTHERN WATER FEATURE

Landscape Architects Hargreaves Associates in
association with Schaffer Barnsley

Construction Abigroup

Engineering Ove Arup & Partners,
Barry Webb and Associates

Project Management Ley Reynolds,
Wilde and Woollard Pacific

Acting as an extension of Olympic Boulevard, the
Northern Water Feature continues the Homebush
Bay theme of connecting the present with the
natural and industrial past of the site. When
visitors tire of the relentless energy and activity of
the sporting complex they can stroll down the
Boulevard into this sculpted artificial landscape
which is simultaneously monumental and delicate.
The 112 metres of the Haslams Pier leads the
visitor away from the 21st century and back into
the timeless history of the wetlands. Artist, Ari
Purhonen, has subtly intervened with the pier to
draw attention to the invisible activity below where
run-off water is purified by natural processes.

Architect Tonkin Zulaikha Architects
Construction Multiplex and Abigroup
Engineering Barry Webb and Associates, and Taylor Thomson Whitting
Project Management NSW Department of Public Works and Services

PUBLIC DOMAIN LIGHTING PYLONS

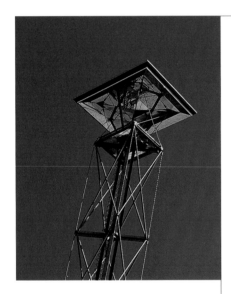

Designed to 'furnish' the Olympic Plaza, a series of nineteen light and information pylons define the western side of Olympic Boulevard and the vast open spaces in front of Stadium Australia and the SuperDome. These 30 metre high pylons impart a sense of scale and orientation when seen against the gigantic size of the two main stadia. They are not intended to be politely urbane street lamps but instead dynamic and useful structural devices that complement the engineering bravado nearby.

Each pylon base is defined as a massive concrete leg supporting a counterbalanced steel tower. The pylons also evoke a more direct memory of the electricity towers which used to dominate this former industrial landscape. At each pylon base are services such as telephones, recycling/rubbish stations, information, toilets, kiosks, water bubblers and seating, as well as a name and date plate of a previous Olympic host city. The counter-balancing arm of the pylon tower supports a 15 metre square canopy of solar collectors. This cantilevered canopy functions both as power generator and shade structure for weary spectators below.

Indicating their solar function, all the pylons lean away from the stadia towards true north and each is topped with a square-multifaceted light reflector. Floodlights are shone upwards onto a faceted mirror which diffuses the spread of light below. When seen in succession along Olympic Boulevard, these pylons create a powerful urban rhythm. At night, their effect is dramatic, with blue neon lights creating an ethereal atmosphere.

PHILIP GOAD

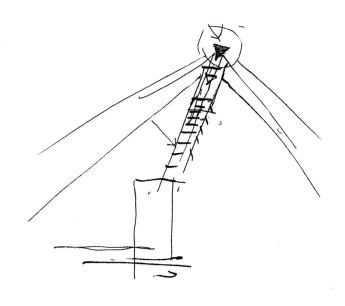

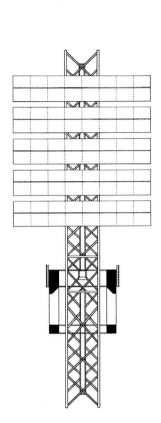

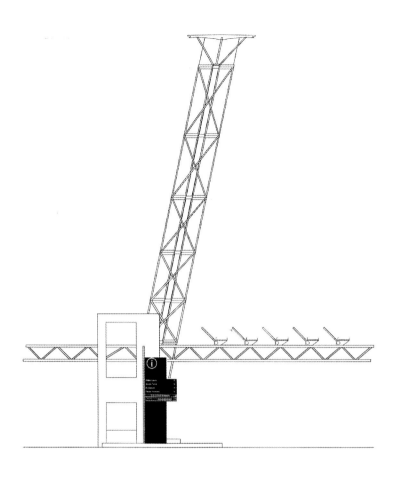

Nineteen light and information pylons line the western side of Olympic Boulevard. By their scale they help pedestrians relate to the monumental proportions of Stadium Australia and the SuperDome on the one hand and the vast expanse of the Boulevard on the other. They also serve visitors at the practical level of providing telephones, recycling and refuse stations, information, toilets, kiosks, water fountains and seating. During the day, the cantilevered canopy of solar collectors acts as shade, while at night their floodlights shine upwards into faceted mirrors to diffuse the light below.

Architect Durbach Block Murcutt
Construction Commercial Building Group
Engineering Ove Arup & Partners
Project Management Gutteridge Haskins & Davey

PUBLIC DOMAIN AMENITIES BLOCKS

A glance across the range of Olympic facilities, both at Homebush and elsewhere, reveals the pre-eminence of steel as a construction material for large structures in contemporary Australia. Its skeletal qualities and ease of fabrication is evident in the delivery of the range of Olympic venues well within time and within budget.

The three amenities blocks strung on the southern side of the Homebush site are a sly take on their surrounding buildings. Small enough to be free of the engineering demands of the larger structures, they toy with the construction methods and the aesthetics of their larger neighbours. Consisting of a series of portal frames over soberly planned masonry-walled amenities blocks, the architects have imbued these buildings with several witty and insightful characteristics. Knowing that the great challenge of large buildings lies in the roof structure, these modest blocks too have their engineered roofs leaping clear of the lower structure. Mindful of the economies to be gained from using identical repetitive components, the blocks flaunt their portals where each frame varies from the one adjacent. Critical of the reticence of many public toilets, the amenities blocks draw onlookers to their bright colours and taut fabric roofs.

The result goes beyond simply a contrary stance to the Olympic facilities and the steel-framed warehouses which lie over the nearby freeway. Having pulled apart the logic of building, the architects have reassembled the components into a series of engaging experiences. Within the toilets, the translucent roofs provide an unexpected light-filled setting for what is regarded as the most mundane of activities. Outside, the colonnade formed by the portals flares and returns, creating a changing vista through its length and a sculpted object when viewed from afar.

The distinctive forms serve a broader function too. Highly visible by day and even more so at night, when the fabric roofs are lit from within, the blocks will be points of orientation for the vast crowds which will fill the site during the Olympics. They also serve as beacons of intense colour for the site as a whole as it is viewed from the trunk roads and freeway which skirt it.

In many ways a counterpoint to the earnest effort which an undertaking of the scale of the Olympics invariably entails, the amenities blocks serve as carefully crafted latter-day jesters. Through humour, and by flaunting a considered and singular idea of beauty, they reveal aspects of the architecture of the site which might otherwise go unnoticed.

HARRY MARGALIT

The amenities and ticketing building alongside the Aquatic Centre accommodates a compact brief, housing a ticketing office for Olympic parking and some change facilities for Olympic officials. Although small, the building evolved into a complex geometric exercise. The framed and sheeted construction, clad in copper, is an ambitious attempt to produce an evocative form out of simple yet highly malleable building materials. The result, akin to a small green-cloaked roadhouse with a presence beyond its size, stands in quirky contrast to the concrete bulk of the Aquatic Centre. Its singular colour and shape make it a strong visual cue to visitors orienting themselves to the Olympic site and its facilities.

Architect Hassell
Construction Leighton Contractors
Engineering Tierney and Partners
Project Management Gutteridge Haskins & Davey

OLYMPIC PARK RAILWAY STATION

For tens of thousands of spectators arriving at Homebush Bay, the Olympic Park Railway Station will be the first piece of Olympic architecture that they will experience. Located west of the main Olympic Plaza, the station is the focal arrival point and landmark of a close-knit urban agglomeration of buildings that make up the Showgrounds precinct. It is the gateway to the Olympic site, a linear, open-ended and translucent portal above a sleekly detailed incision into the earth. Not part of Sydney's initial bid to stage the 2000 Olympics, the decision to include a rail link to Homebush came about through an international design workshop (1993). The architects were subsequently appointed to examine options for the reintroduction of a heavy rail link to the site and in 1995, the new Master Plan adopted a loop rail link and the recommendation for an underground station in the very centre of the Olympic site. The decision was an urban design master stroke. Now the site's pivotal public transport hub, the Olympic Park Railway Station has already distinguished itself, gaining state and national acclaim in 1998 as recipient of the RAIA's prestigious Sir John Sulman Medal and Sir Zelman Cowen Award. These awards are a tribute to the scheme's clarity, legibility and powerful urban modesty.

The station's designers conceived the building as 'below ground' rather than 'underground'. It was to be an open air structure that would celebrate the act of arrival and departure and give emphasis to two fundamental aspects of the site: the overpowering impression of the sky; and a linear axis – to the east across the mangroves and the distant view of central Sydney, and to the west, to the main Olympic Stadium. Intrinsic to the success of this concept is the fact that the train dips underground 1.5 kilometres before arrival at the Olympic site. Speeding west from Sydney, the distant glimpses of Homebush are made all the more tantalising by disappearing from view altogether before arrival. As a result, immediate visual orientation on arrival was essential. Rather than arrive in a tunnel, the architects intended that passengers alight in an open airy volume, almost as if the 'solid base' of the urban square outside had been folded down 6.5 metres to form a sunken space of public assembly.

Designed to handle crowds of up to 50 000 people per hour arriving and departing, the design of the station platforms becomes the linchpin in the operation of crowd control. At the busiest times of the Olympics, 30 trains per hour are expected to pass through the station. Crowd movement was studied using sophisticated computer programs employed by the London Underground. In Olympic mode, the broader, central platform is dedicated to arrivals while the two side platforms are used for departure only. All access and egress is focused to the west of the station, to the Olympic plaza and the perpendicular axis of the

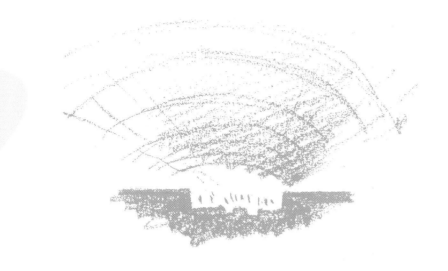

On approach, the train dips underground 1.5 kms from its destination, leaving visitors with a tantalisingly distant view of the complex. Arrival at the station is a series of theatrical moments as visitors are swept upwards from the central platform into the light by flamboyant escalators. From the entry hall, they step out into the Olympic Plaza through a soaring, translucent curved canopy. This architectural fanfare creates a sense of occasion, as the immensity and diversity of the Homebush Bay complex is revealed in one dramatic gesture.

The grand series of eighteen vaulted roof trusses which stretches the 200 metres of the station revive memories of great 19th century railway stations. Like its predecessors, the Olympic Park Railway station combines the florid strength of 12 metre high steel arches with the drama of invading light through the fanned skylights to create a surprisingly delicate structural filigree.

Olympic Boulevard. The platforms are located within the sunken 'box' whose walls are lined with off-white precast concrete panels. A series of stairs and escalators reinforce the linearity of the overall scheme, giving clear messages about directionality, procession and simplified traffic flow. Even the pedestrian ramps are carved as linear slots into the earth. Critical to the overall design was the intention that there not be exhaust systems, that the station be naturally ventilated and lit – in essence that the station conform to the sustainable aims of the Sydney 2000 building and environmental program.

On arrival, one alights beneath the visual highlight of the station, a delicate gently curving canopy. In the tradition of the engineered sheds of the great nineteenth century railway stations, this canopy is translucent, structurally expressive and above all, dramatic. The architects describe its concept as almost 'leaf-like'. A series of single span vaulted roof trusses is repeated eighteen times along the 200 metre length of the station to create a vertebral filigree that is infilled with ribbons of glass and solid roof panels lined underneath with gloss-finished perforated aluminium. Each of the main roof trusses (at 12 metre centres) sits on tapering precast concrete columns which have an ovoid section. Developed initially through the use of paper models and then refined through wind-tunnel testing at the University of Sydney, the arched steel frames form a concertina of folds. Skylights are formed by a line of continuous glazing along the ridge of the vaults. Reflected light then

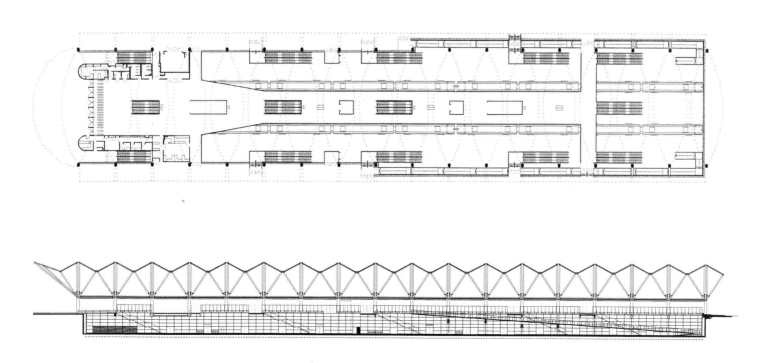

The main single-span roof trusses each sit on imposing tapered pre-cast concrete columns articulating inwards across the void of the arrival and departure platforms. The trusses support the pod-like pitched glass panels of the skylights together with the solid roof sections which are lined underneath with gloss-finished perforated aluminium.

The skeletal roof structure of the Olympic Park Railway Station provided a spectacular perspective during construction. Each ribbed section was delivered in two halves by a massive mobile crane and put into place as a segment of an infinitely repetitive grand space. For a short time, this fanning vista of steel filigree was a re-creation of the great transparent iron and glass structures of the nineteenth century.

illuminates the underside of the canopy while at night, artificial light is thrown up onto the underside of the canopy. The gunnel-like shape of each truss, like a series of upturned skiffs, is emphasised with this evocative lighting scheme. Seen together though, the station becomes a long luminous parasol. This beautifully resolved roof then extends as a flaring curved canopy to the west, a welcome embrace of the main public space at ground level. A secondary canopy, flat and continuous, with glazed strips at the structural supports, runs the length of the station on the north and south sides and a series of shading baffles feathers its outermost edge. At ground level, this canopy is low and humanly scaled. At the base of the glazed barrier, there is even a concrete sill wide enough to become a seat. Inside on the platform, the spatial sensation is completely different. With the arched structure above, the twenty metre high space is grand, tall and appropriately breathtaking.

Seen through the trees, the organic analogy of a leaf floating above a solid base echoes gracefully Jørn Utzon's brilliant concept for the Sydney Opera House, that of a cloud floating above a plateau or platform of functional purpose. One of the very few public buildings in Sydney to extend Utzon's ideas in a meaningful way and into an entirely new and different urban context, the Olympic Park Railway Station heralds not just entry to the Games but a reaffirmation of the possibilities of defining a new urban architecture for Sydney.

PHILIP GOAD

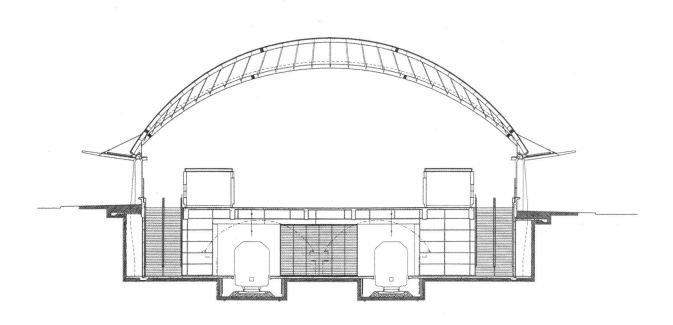

Architect Woods Bagot
Construction Abigroup
Engineering Taylor Thomson Whitting
Project Management NSW Department of Public Works & Services

SYDNEY INTERNATIONAL REGATTA CENTRE, PENRITH LAKES ROWING SHEDS

Venue for Olympic rowing, sprint and slalom canoe/kayak events, the Penrith Lakes lie serenely at the foothills of the Blue Mountains, 44 kilometres west of Homebush Bay. Stage I of the project involved infilling a former sand and gravel quarry to create a tranquil lake environment. The site was extensively regraded, landscaped and planted to create a unique international boating venue which will eventually form part of a 2000 hectare public recreation area of seven lakes. The new buildings at Penrith are sensitive to this transformed landscape; modest linear pavilions respectful of the land and deferring to the water.

Sitting on an island between the artificially created warm-up lake to the north and competition course to the south, the Sydney International Regatta Centre includes a series of three structures: start and finishing towers and timing huts; a pavilion with grandstand seating; and two boatsheds. The course itself is 2300 metres long, 130 metres wide with a consistent five metre depth along its length. The rock coated and wave absorbing banks as well as the introduced planting are designed to ensure that virtually no assisted or negative wind and currents effects would occur. Nine lane rowing events are held over 2000 metres and twelve lane canoeing races take place over 200, 500 and 1000 metres.

The pavilion and rowing sheds were designed as an interconnecting complex joined on-grade by a pedestrian walkway with zig-zagging ramps to riverbank level. A party atmosphere of a regatta was a written requirement for the pavilion and its surrounding terraces. Auguste Renoir's painting 'The Boating Party', which depicts revelling picnickers on Paris's River Seine, provided the perfect image. The new pavilion was thus designed to be informal with its terraced edges blurred to merge with the grass, the site for picnics and where cheering crowds could gather.

Overlooking the competition course and located on top of an artificially created ridge, the pavilion was designed as an open structure with a large overhanging pergola-like roof. The pavilion itself contains a broad open shaded terrace, a dining room, office and other amenities. On the lake side and beneath the flat pergola canopy the bank has been terraced and gently descends across grass to a lakeside promenade and eventually a shoreline of river pebbles. Three of the terraces have timber decks with slide-out seating for 1000 spectators. Unlike a conventional grandstand, this pergola has motorised fabric awnings. When seated beneath it, spectators could be watching the races under a white umbrella. The overall design was dictated by the clarity of intersection of the steel frame of the skillion roofed pavilion and the steel frame of the giant pergola. This pavilion is thus a study in a site-responsive building section, a minimal material palette, structural simplicity, and above all, a composition which defers to the horizontal nature of the gently rippling course below.

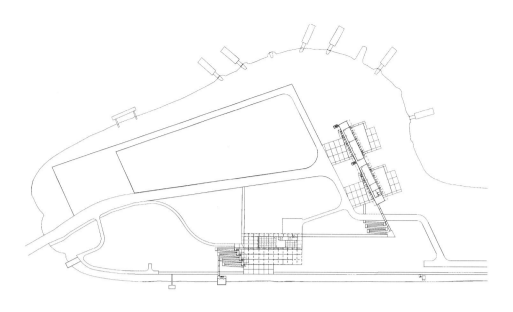

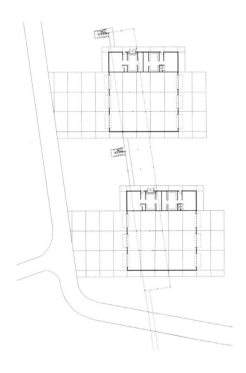

The two boatsheds which face the warm-up lake follow this same tautly controlled material and structural palette. Each shed, divisible into three bays, has racking and storage for up to 80 boats as well as workshop space. The sheds, spaced apart at ground level to provide extra storage, are joined overhead by an open breezeway of vertical timber slats. The upper level, expressed as a separate linear block canted at an angle to the sheds below, houses gymnasium spaces, medical support and meeting rooms. In Olympic mode, management and officials will occupy this space. The west facing wall has a series of angled struts to the deep roof eaves with timber battens providing extra shade protection. In Olympic mode, this entire grassed area to the north of the sheds will be covered with tents for showers, change rooms and boat storage. PHILIP GOAD

Architect Conybeare Morrison & Partners
Construction Cooinda Constructions Australia
Engineering Northrop Holmes Engineers
Project Management NSW Department of Public Works and Services

SYDNEY INTERNATIONAL REGATTA CENTRE, PENRITH LAKES
FINISH TOWER

C onstructed as Stage II of the Regatta Centre are the start and finish towers and the timing huts which all sit partly over the water. These award-winning structures have gently curved roofs, broad eaves and tapering rafters. The exposed steel construction, with generous glazing and corrugated steel cladding set the architectural palette for the other buildings on the site.

The Finish Tower is the control point of the whole Regatta Centre. It has four levels, the topmost of which accommodates the photofinish cameras while lower levels provide space for up to nine judges, timing devices, commentary and the Regatta Control Office. Its curved roof form, while notionally echoing the rise of nearby hills, has a string of solar panels which provide power for timing equipment and other needs of the Regatta Centre.

PHILIP GOAD

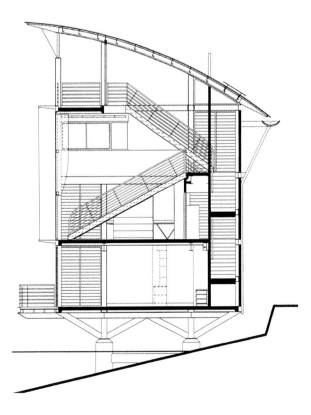

Architect Grose Bradley
Construction D G Sundin and Co
Engineering Pacific Power International
Project Management Pacific Power International

PENRITH WHITEWATER STADIUM

Designed for use as a public white water sports facility after the Games, the Penrith Whitewater Stadium is a totally artificial construction. Even the water is engineered to bubble and surge for 300 metres providing a demanding course for all Olympic kayak and canoeing slalom events. Boats assemble in a lower pond before loading individually onto a conveyor belt which transports them to an upper pond. From here, the boats make their way to the foaming torrent of the whitewater channel. The water is powered by massive generators in a pumping station at the lower pond level, like a miniature hydro-electric power station in reverse. With moveable obstacles and variable water flows, competitors will hurtle down a slalom course of 20 to 25 gates set in turbulent water with at least six gates to be manoeuvred in an upstream direction.

Servicing the whitewater course is a wedge-shaped building whose roof follows the slope of the land. The building is totally unadorned – concrete blocks, galvanized steel beams and columns, cyclone wire and perforated metal are the budget-determined material choices. But given these limits, the architects have been inventive. Ramps for the disabled run up the slope on either side of the simple shed and, beneath its roof, become the organising device for the building's plan and structure. At the top of the wedge, on passing through a breezeway, one arrives at a generous open terrace, as if beneath a giant sloping verandah. A zig-zag of steel pipe and cyclone wire infill is the prosaic boundary to the carpark beyond. At the bottom of the wedge is boat storage where walls and aircraft doors sheeted in expanded metal give a level of transparency to a volume whose height has been dictated by the length of a kayak. Even with this rigorous and lean economy, this tough little building makes direct but sensitive gestures to the land. It is the perfect accompaniment to an equally tough water course nearby. PHILIP GOAD

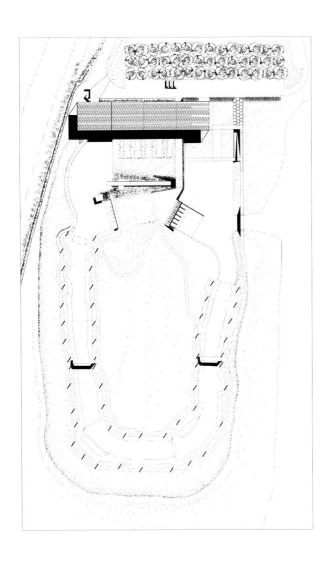

Looking across the artificially-constructed warm-up lake at the Regatta Centre, the Penrith Whitewater Stadium is to the far right of the picture at the north-east corner of the lake. The course itself is a looped 300m concrete-lined channel with earth banks for spectators. It is the first separate whitewater slalom canoe course to be constructed in Australia and will continue after the Games as a community recreational facility and venue for official competitions.

Architect Group GSA
Construction Belmadar Construction
Engineering Sinclair Knight Merz
Project Management NSW Department of Public Works and Services

SYDNEY INTERNATIONAL SHOOTING CENTRE, CECIL PARK

The new Sydney International Shooting Centre on the Cumberland Plain is focused on a linear building incised into a sloping site. The venue's major element is a gun-barrel concourse which unifies the complex and runs for 250 metres, the entire length of the building. Located off this walkway are the individual shooting bays for 10m indoor, 25m and 50m open ranges and, located to the right of the entry terrace, a finals range which has adjustable sliding walls to form either a 25 or 50 metre range. There is also a shotgun range. Viewing terraces are located immediately below the entire length of the walkway and the venue has a total capacity of 10 000 spectators.

From the perpendicular approach drive lined by a low grey stone gabion wall, the Sydney International Shooting Centre appears as a horizontal line floating above the grassland. It stands in stark contrast to the sculptural beauty of existing mature eucalypts scattered over the landscape. This line is a cantilevering tilted roof supported off a massive steel girder truss which runs the length of the building. The entry terrace is airy and open to distant views of the countryside beyond. The excitement of the building comes through the section and the repetition of architectural elements, in particular the cantilevering galvanised steel roof beams which form a staccato silver salute as one looks along the seemingly infinite length of the concourse.

While the building follows a rigorous order of twenty one 12 metre modular bays, the material choice and the play of natural light provide a textural and visual counterpoint. The spartan palette is of weathered zinc and rough sawn vertical and horizontal timber infill slabs. The same feeling is engendered by bunker like off-form concrete sound baffle walls around the ranges which impart an evocative patina of age to robust acoustic dampening forms whose future will be studded with bullet holes. By contrast, the girder truss, sheeted in translucent fibreglass and the rough sawn timbers battens overhead in the competition ranges contribute a soft, almost delicate light to the interior. Located in the grasslands below the complex are trap and skeet ranges, which like the complex above, nestle comfortably into the landscape. PHILIP GOAD

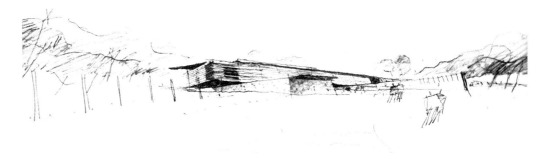

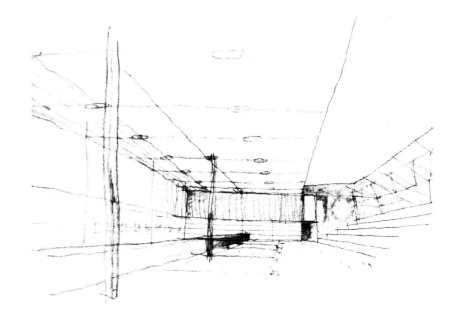

The Sydney International Shooting Centre will
continue to be a valuable facility for New South Wales
after the Olympic Games. It will be a venue for local,
national and international competitions and includes
10m, 25m and 50m ranges, three trap layouts,
covered spectator facilities and support facilities.

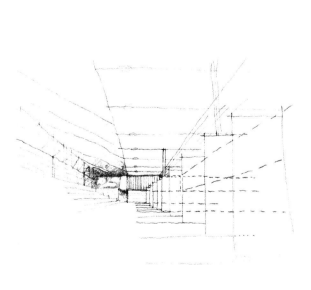

Architect RyderSJPH, a consortium of Ryder Associates and SJPH Design
Partnership
Construction Walter Construction Group
Engineering Ove Arup & Partners
Project Management Australian Pacific Projects

DUNCAN GRAY VELODROME, BANKSTOWN

This interesting and structurally innovative building was the result of a design competition held in 1992. The architects then adapted their winning design as the site moved from Homebush to its new location at The Crest, an 85 hectare recreation area at Bankstown, a nearby suburb where it will become part of a new regional sporting complex. The stadium's distinctive feature is its roof, likened by some to the shell of a tortoise, but more properly inspired by the aerodynamic shape of the toroid or, in simple terms, a cyclist's racing helmet. Another analogy, more geometric in concept, is that the toroid form comes from the double radii of a bicycle tyre's inner tube. This roof, a collaborative design effort by the architects and engineers, provides a totally free span and floats over the oval track and terraced seating. The roof structure is essentially a framed shell composed of parallel arches, all of which have an identical curvature. An elliptical ring beam ties the arches which are held apart by a lattice of diagonal bracing. Outside, dramatically raked V-shaped steel props support the roof off the ground, and in places these struts slice through concrete floors creating dynamic elliptical cutouts. Designed to maximise natural lighting and ventilation, a series of adjustable ellipsoid-shaped louvres overhead enables the correct ambience for naturally lit racing conditions while perimeter window louvres and adjustable wall openings combine with roof vents to allow for thermal stack/cross flow ventilation.

Inside, the visual focus is twofold: above the diagonal latticework of the roof with its encircling light gantry, and below the golden hue of the 250 metre baltic timber track. Unlike Olympic velodromes at Barcelona and Atlanta where the tracks were either temporary or plywood, this venue's track is permanent and constructed down to the last millimetre to ensure the smoothest and most accurate profile. Supported by rows of timber trusses, and with a surface of skew nailed baltic pine strips, the track has all the qualities of a perfectly rigid and beautifully constructed timber boat. Normally the velodrome will seat 3000 spectators but in Olympic mode, temporary seating will double the venue's capacity. During events, officials, medal ceremonies and warm-up pens for the cyclists will occupy the middle of the arena.

The stadium's unusual roof form extends to the north to provide foyer, concessions and service spaces, and it is this extra space which results in its eccentric shape. In non-Olympic mode, an internal promenade encircles the stadium and is tucked inside beneath the terraced seating. To cope with crowd movement during the Olympics and to double circulation space, a special external promenade is being constructed around the velodrome's perimeter. PHILIP GOAD

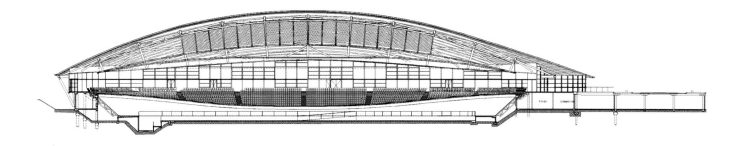

The result of a collaboration between the architects and engineers, the Velodrome's roof floats above the 250m oval cycling track and terraced seating and is designed to maximise natural light and ventilation. Inside there is a dynamic interplay between the diagonal latticework of the roof and the baltic timber track. Unlike previous Olympic velodromes at Barcelona and Atlanta, which were either temporary or made of plywood, this track is permanent and provides the smoothest possible profile. After the Olympics, removal of temporary seating will return the velodrome's capacity to 3000 and provide an internal promenade underneath the roof overhang and terraced seating. As well as cycling, the facility will be a venue for concerts and indoor sports such as volleyball, hockey and basketball.

Architect Equus 2000 Pty Ltd Architects; Joint venture of Scott Carver,
Timothy Court & Co and SJPH Design Partnership
Construction Lipman
Engineering Kinhill
Project Management Incoll Management

THE SYDNEY INTERNATIONAL EQUESTRIAN CENTRE, HORSLEY PARK

West of the city, in the semi-rural belt of market gardens and smallholdings which are fast passing to suburban development, lies Sydney's new premier equestrian facility. Comprising over 80 hectares of native and regenerated bushland, the centre forms an important component of a larger Western Sydney Regional Park.

As befits a sport with rural roots, much of the artistry in the design of the centre lies in the kilometres of endurance roads and tracks and in the cross country course. The two major structures also take their cues from a rural tradition. The stables buildings, which will house up to 340 horses during the Olympics, consist of two large roofs stepped and vented against the heat in a location some distance from the sea. Although the majority of the events are held outdoors, competitors are protected against the vagaries of weather by the enclosed 70 x 35 metre training hall with raked spectator seating. Its roof is spanned by arched trusses, whilst a series of secondary cleated frames allow the roof form to sit away from the upper chord of the truss. The roof is thus only part barrel, its northern section cascading to form a series of strip rooflights. This technique of bringing light through the roof has a long history in Australian rural building, with at least one fine example, a shearing barn at Uralla in the New England region of northern New South Wales, dating from the mid-nineteenth century.

Surrounding these buildings are the range of facilities for competition and training: lunging rings, numerous sand arenas and five grass hacking arenas. The main arena, for showjumping and dressage, has permanent seats and banks for 5000 spectators, but this will be expanded to 20 000 for the Olympics with the aid of temporary grandstands.

The extensive effort to re-establish native woodland on the site is backed up by an integrated stormwater management and filtration system. This system aids in minimising flood damage and improving water quality with the use of settling ponds and a wetland filtration system. These measures collectively will restore to the site some of the variety of vegetation and stability of landscape which existed before the area was given over to farming a century and a half ago. Also integral to the identity of the area is the recognition and preservation of fourteen significant sites recording evidence of Aboriginal life and custom prior to colonisation. HARRY MARGALIT

The Equestrian Centre at Horsley Park forms part of the larger Western Sydney Regional Park. It will be a permanent home for equestrian events, but extensive parkland improvement has also created a new community recreational facility by rehabilitating the woodlands and vegetation previously lost to farming.

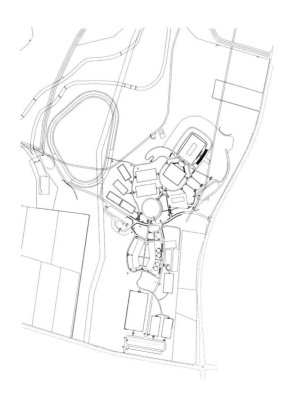

SYDNEY SHOWGROUNDS

For almost two centuries The Royal Easter Show has been part of Sydney's agricultural and social fabric. Scene of cattle shows, show jumping and parading prize bulls, its home for most of this time was in Paddington, an inner suburb of Sydney. It now has a new home at Homebush Bay where the Sydney Showgrounds, designed in three precincts by three teams of architects, is spread over 30 hectares. These new showgrounds include more than 140 000 square metres of animal pavilions and exhibition halls, as well as a showring. In keeping with the 1995 Homebush Masterplan, this collection of buildings has been developed as a tightly packed urban environment, a virtual town of narrow streets and large sheds. In September 2000, the Sydney Showgrounds will take on a totally different function. It will be a vital precinct housing not just numerous indoor Olympic sports but it will also be the venue for Olympic baseball and provide vast open plan accommodation for the world's media. PHILIP GOAD

Architect Ancher Mortlock & Woolley
Construction Thiess Contractors
Engineering Ove Arup & Partners
Project Management Australian Pacific Projects

SYDNEY SHOWGROUNDS
EXHIBITION HALLS

Dubbed the 'Australian Pantheon', the dome of the Sydney Showgrounds Exhibition Halls is the most striking feature of the linear series of exhibition halls that will be the venue for Olympic badminton, handball, rhythmic gymnastics, and preliminaries for the volleyball and basketball. These large span halls were designed with two functions in mind: Easter Show exhibitions and indoor Olympic sports. This resulted in spans exceeding 67 metres, heights of 25 to 35 metres and 22 000 square metre open floor area.

The four halls – one circular and three rectangular – can be used separately or as one uninterrupted 312 metre long space. The dome, a tribute to the circular Banquet Hall at the old Moore Park Showgrounds, is 97 metres in diameter, 42 metres high, and mighty in size, seating 10 000 spectators. It is the dominating feature of the Sydney Showgrounds, the largest structure of its kind in the southern hemisphere and the only public showground space to be airconditioned. The other three halls accommodate 7000 spectators for handball, 5000 for volleyball and 5000 for badminton and rhythmic gymnastics. As part of the project's ESD ambitions, laminated plantation timbers were used for all principal structural members with steel used for jointing and tension members, as well as wall framing and columns. Instead of Pier Luigi Nervi's reinforced concrete filigree dome for the Palazzo del Sport at the Rome Olympics (1960), also an attempt at a minimal surface, the architects opted for a green solution. The exquisite interlaced web of the tensioned dome roof is thus a composite structure of steel and timber, one of the world's most significant such structures since the Lillehammer buildings for the Winter Olympics in Norway (1994). The construction strategy was to build, on the ground, the 27 metre diameter top ring first and then erect the dome progressively. The structure was jacked up as each ring was constructed and it was, according to the architects, rather like 'the construction of a crinoline skirt', a series of conical surfaces, which, when pieced together, formed a dome.

Linking the dome and Exhibition Halls to the west and south is a red brick colonnaded administration building, an urban face to the railway square and Olympic Plaza Park, while to the north there is a fabric verandah roof where the halls can open up to a sun-filled public thoroughfare. PHILIP GOAD

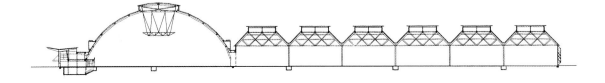

The Sydney Showgrounds Exhibition Halls consist of a series of halls which can be used separately or as one uninterrupted 312 metre long space. The dual purpose of the halls as both an Olympic venue and a Royal Easter Show exhibition site required a building of considerable size containing large uninterrupted floor spaces, created by the use of immense structural spans.

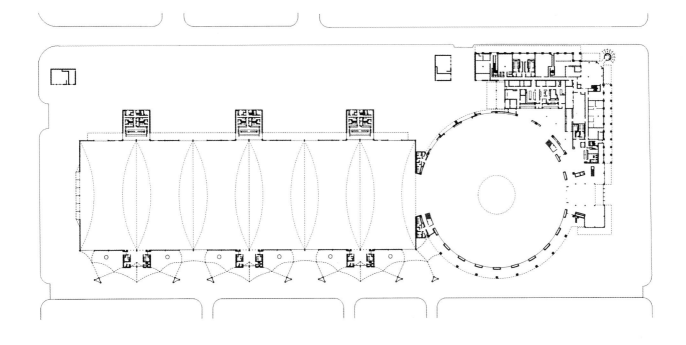

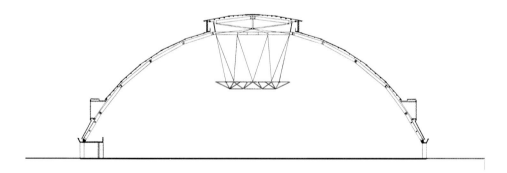

The soaring dome of the Sydney Showgrounds Exhibition Halls doffs its hat to the dome of the circular Banquet Hall at the old Moore Park Showgrounds in recognition of the Royal Agricultural Society's long relationship with its old venue. The interlaced web of the tensioned dome is the largest structure of its kind in the southern hemisphere and stands as a triumphal completion point to the linear series of exhibition halls which make up the complex.

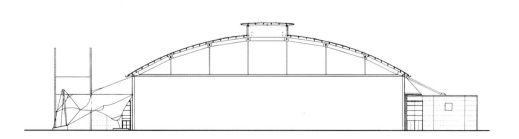

Architect Cox Richardson, Peddle Thorp,
Conybeare Morrison, as CPTC
Construction AW Edwards and Transfield
Engineering Hyder Consulting
Project Management Australian Pacific Projects

SYDNEY SHOWGROUNDS
SHOWRING (BASEBALL)

A different team of architects were responsible for designing pavilions for Dogs, Cats, the Woodchop Arena and the Sydney Showgrounds Showring. In Olympic mode, the first three structures will function as service facilities. The Cats Pavilion is a miniature parody of its larger neighbour, the Sydney Showgrounds Exhibition Halls, while the Woodchop Arena is a refreshingly prosaic compound which features log poles and rudimentary stepped concrete seating. By contrast, the Sydney Showgrounds Showring is decidedly festive. With its six bright red supporting masts (which double as light towers) and its grandstand canopy, made up of five inverted wedge-shaped conical segments, the Sydney Showgrounds Showring has a dual function: a baseball stadium all year round and, during Easter and other times, animal parades, show jumping, dressage and polo. Intended as a dynamic contrast to the iconic Exhibition Hall dome, the Sydney Showgrounds Showring is one of the more lyrically shaped structures of Homebush. At the batting end (when used for baseball) and beneath the canopy with its shallow humped profile (analogous to a series of baseball caps) is grandstand seating for 12 000 spectators. Grassed banks to the arena's north-east take seating capacity to 20 000 during the Easter Show. The arena's egg-like double ellipse plan was determined by Sydney Showgrounds requirements (an oval) and the shape of a baseball pitch (diamond). Five distinct articulated bays were introduced to allow vistas and easy permeability through the stand, locus points also for vertical and lateral circulation, services reticulation and the articulation of the striking red masts which drop almost to a point at ground level. PHILIP GOAD

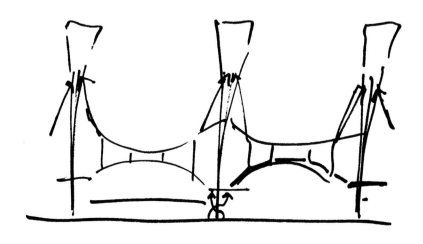

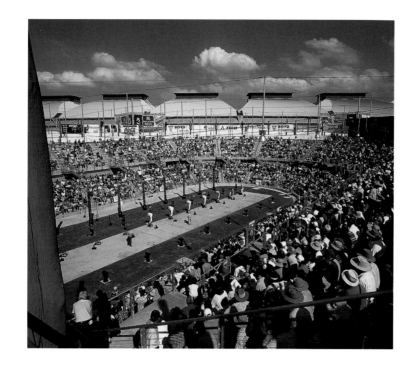

Probably nothing epitomises the annual Royal Easter Show more than the wood chopping competition. It is a direct link back to a past agricultural era, celebrating a craft now largely lost but surviving as an art. In the context of the most modern sporting and exhibition complex in Australia, the wood chopping competition continues as a symbol of Australia's agrarian origins. This is reflected in the way the venue references the vernacular tradition in Australian building, especially some venues at the old RAS Showrounds in Moore Park, with its subtly pitched corrugated iron roof and overhang supported by expressed timber columns to create a sheltered colonnade.

Architect Pavilion Architects, a consortium of Scott Carver,

SJPH Design Partnership, and Timothy Court & Co

Construction Baulderstone and Belmadar Construction

Engineering SCP Consulting

Project Management Australian Pacific Projects

SYDNEY SHOWGROUNDS
ANIMAL PAVILIONS

The remaining pavilions which house animals during the Easter Show, are used as examination spaces at other times. During Olympic mode, they become temporary home to 5 500 members of the world's media. In Paralympic mode, these same pavilions will be venues for judo, goalball, boccia, volleyball, basketball preliminaries, powerlifting, rugby and fencing. The entire roof structure has been designed around heat and smoke rising; obviating the need for sprinklers (hence massive budget savings), maximising daylight but minimising glare and heat gain. When transformed, the vast interior becomes the Olympic media centre, fitted out and visually zoned into Australian themes. PHILIP GOAD

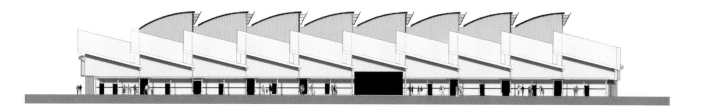

The massive fabric vents running the length of the animal pavilions are simultaneously functional and referential. These udder-like exhaust funnels draw heat and fumes up through the roof, and provide a distinctive anthropomorphic vista.

Architect Alexander Tzannes Associates

Construction – Stage One: Australian Wharf & Bridge Constructions

Stage Two: Gledhill Constructions

Engineering Taylor Lauder Bersten

Project Management Gutteridge Haskins Davey

HOMEBUSH BAY FERRY WHARF

The Parramatta River is the extension of Sydney's great centrepiece, the harbour, drawing it westwards from the city to the old heart of Parramatta. The harbour and the river divide the city into north and south, and their linking has given Sydney two of its most visible structures, the Harbour Bridge and the Gladesville Bridge. In recent years the river has been rediscovered as a commuter passageway, as its shores are reclaimed from industrial uses.

The Homebush Bay Ferry Wharf is the first in a series of planned new wharf structures on the river run. It is the connection point for water transport to the Olympic site, a vital mode of travel considering the loads which road and rail are expected to carry for the duration of the Olympics and Paralympics. Given the iconic status of Sydney Harbour and the Parramatta River, the wharf carries a significance perhaps greater than its passenger load would suggest.

The design of the structures which comprise the wharf are representative of a certain classicism which has emerged in Sydney architecture within the last two decades. It is characterised by a clarity of line, and a desire to reduce buildings to simple uncompromising constituent elements with considered joints and junctions. Thus the two long perpendicular vaults which form the basic structure are kept apart by a smaller roof piece, the better to maintain their consistent edges and ends. Great attention has been paid to fixings and joins, such that every visible detail has a mathematical rigour. This underlying care in proportioning the building allows it to sit comfortably next to the shade structure which provides overflow shelter, as the two are linked by the evident and uncluttered rhythms of their repetitive forms.

This classical approach has resonance beyond the structures themselves. It resembles the logic of boats, where simplicity and durability prevail. These, in turn, have been long-admired qualities in the Australian rural tradition, where elegance meets necessity in a finely-judged solution.

A more overt maritime connection is evoked through the timber-slatted waiting benches and the muted colour scheme. The building also conforms to the tradition of Sydney Harbour ferry wharves, where the structures simply aid embarking and disembarking with the minimum of fuss, provide shelter from the rain and allow some low-key moments: a spot of fishing or a brief repose at sunset while walking the dog. HARRY MARGALIT

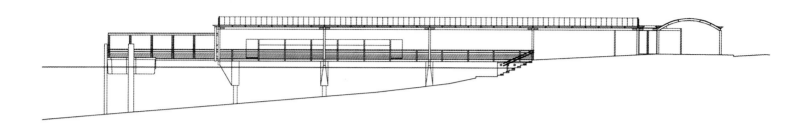

The Homebush Bay Ferry Wharf is the first in a series of new wharf structures on the Parramatta River planned to satisfy the increasing popularity of this mode of transport with urban commuters. The rhythmic shade structures seen here, provide overflow shelter for embarking ferry passengers during periods of high traffic during major sporting events.

Architect Ancher Mortlock & Woolley
Construction Kell & Rigby and Abigroup
Engineers Connell Wagner
Project Management Sinclair Knight Merz

STATE HOCKEY CENTRE

E legant, even delicate with its bonnet-like roof, the State Hockey Centre is the venue for one of Australia's premier Olympic sports. The site was conceived by the architect as a huge flat elliptical terrace with a pitch recessed into it. The result is an open air arena with a covered grandstand on the west side. In Olympic mode, the complex will accommodate 15 000 spectators: 10 000 on temporary seating, 1500 on permanent terraced seating, 1500 in the grandstand and 2000 on grassed banks created by removing earth from the site to form the level pitch (with its orientation of 15° east of north). The pitch seating, curved at the corners and sides, has optimum sightlines and a media and officials corridor lies between the terraced seating and pitch boundary wall. Four light towers, poised like giant desk lamps, lean toward the pitch, each angled to minimise peripheral light spill over the brilliant green synthetic pitch. Sitting discreetly above this basin-like arena, the red brick grandstand with a shimmering horizontal veil of expanded metal on its entry side has, directly beneath it, three levels of player, administrative and spectator facilities. Its design emphasises themes of tension and compression. The finely detailed banded brick base structure is symmetrically planned. By contrast, held tautly above it, is a lightweight steel roof completely separate from the massive building below. Suspended from a central mast, this inverted catenary roof is made up of five planes held down at either end. Entirely different geometries inform the visual separateness of roof and grandstand structure – one is dynamic, the other static. While the State Hockey Centre might appear diminutive, it is one of the first Olympic stadia to be closely visible from the freeway, an incidental role to its function certainly, but highly significant as a finely resolved foretaste to the Homebush Bay complex. PHILIP GOAD

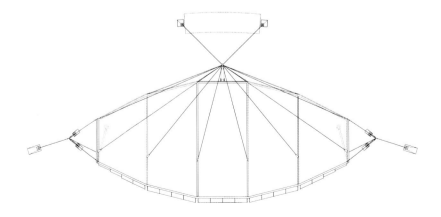

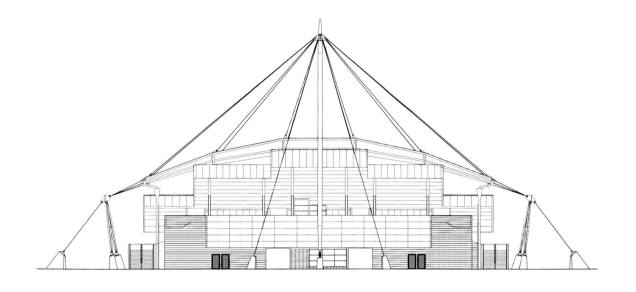

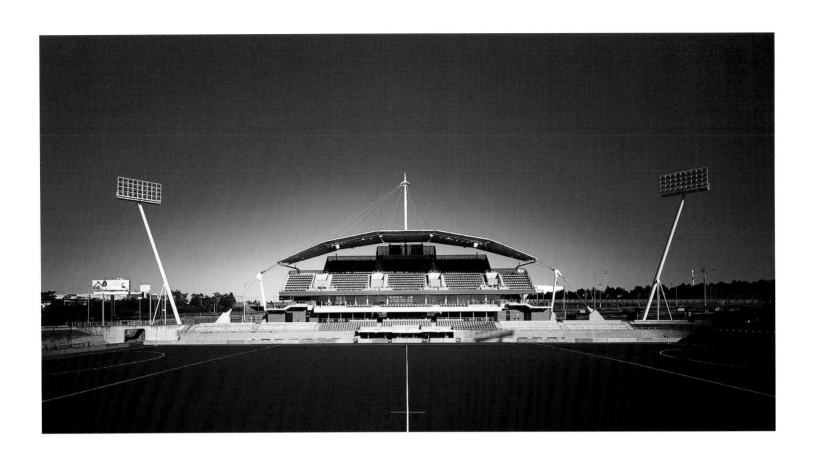

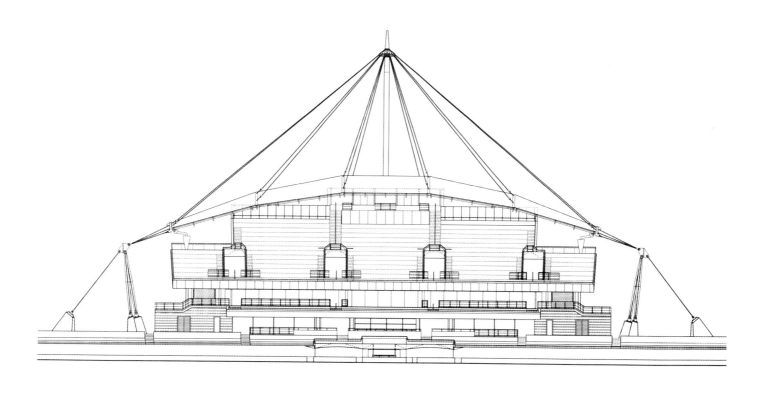

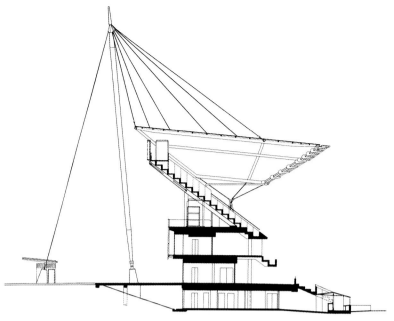

A southern view of the grandstand at the State Hockey Centre reveals a series of contrasts which give the building a compelling sense of dynamism. The grandstand itself sits decisively on its base. But above it, indeed quite separate from it, the lightweight steel roof threatens to fly away, restrained only by the 45 degree supporting cables fanning out from an angled mast at the rear of the building. Adding to the effect of a range of components working in co-operative tension are the contrasting red brickwork of the grandstand wall, unpainted concrete staunchions and red, silver metal and white painted steel elements.

Architect Philip Cox Richardson Taylor and Peddle Thorp
Construction Civil & Civic
Engineering Connell Wagner
Project Management Civil & Civic

SYDNEY INTERNATIONAL ATHLETIC CENTRE

One of the first buildings completed at Homebush in the bid to secure Sydney as the location for the 2000 Olympics. The Sydney International Athletic Centre, finished in September 1993 comprises a 15 000 spectator athletics venue that will be used as the main warm-up track during the Games. There are two major components: a main competition arena (for pre and post Games events) and a warm-up track. The larger of the two tracks has a roofed grandstand seating 2500 spectators while a further 2500 fixed seats are provided with 10 000 temporary seats able to be installed during the Games on top of the curved earth berms that surround the larger arena. This theme of landscaped banks has been, for more than twenty years, a consistent feature of Philip Cox's philosophy of reducing the scale of large stadia and providing wind protection to the arenas within. To achieve this, 40 000 cubic metres of earth excavated during construction was reused for the Centre's grassed and landscaped embankments. The complex is thus not aggressive in its use of structure nor overpowering in size. The curved grandstand with its delicate and innovative cable-stayed arched roof and two steel-framed masts provides a dynamic visual counterpoint to the earthbound structures at eye level. The grandstand roof tilts forward and a catenary cable curved over its entire length provides restraint from uplifting wind forces. The masts which support this roof double as light standards. Together with the Aquatic Centre, the Sydney International Athletic Centre forms a precinct of sporting structures with landscape curving in plan and undulating in contour. PHILIP GOAD

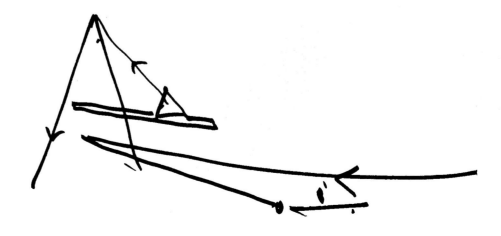

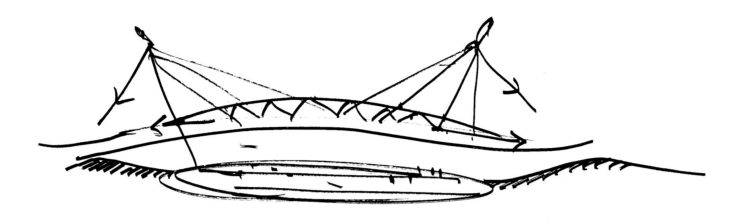

The Athletics Centre viewed from the northern terraced seating demonstrates a continuation and progression of the approach to sporting architecture first implemented by Philip Cox at Canberra's National Athletics Stadium in the 1970s. A combination of smoothly curved and inclined berms used for spectator seating, with dramatically angled supporting masts for the grandstands, which here double as lighting towers. This sinuous integration of topographical landscaping and an architecture with a distinctive nautical profile has now become a standard typology for Australian sporting venues.

Architect Stutchbury & Pape
Construction Cooinda Constructions Australia
Engineering The Structural Design Group
Project Management NSW Department of Public Works & Services

SYDNEY INTERNATIONAL ARCHERY PARK

At first inspection, the archery centre appears as a set of discrete components clearly delineated: the sheeted fly roof over a series of box-like cubicles, the broad swathe of lawn terminated by dark-green mangroves, and two flanking bands of poles planted at regular intervals which diminish in height towards the target end.

Closer inspection reveals an ensemble of building and landscaping with a deep concern for the poetic potential of the facility and the activity it houses. Much as poetry within language aims for a wide resonance with an economy of means, the archery centre has a range of resonances and associations which belie its modest extent. The first of these is clearly the ancient sport of archery, which despite its modern array of counterweights and pulleys still operates at a velocity discernible to the unassisted eye. Arrows sail through the air in trajectories determined by a complex physics still susceptible to wind and weather. The centre, despite being of materials and a form of construction which favours the economy inherent in repetition, responds to the imagery of archery in a variety of ways. The first is in the flanking poles, the sloping plane which they describe corresponding to the diminishing energy which the arrow carries through its flight. The roof structure of the building reveals another more literal allusion in the notched upper ends of the tilted roof beams, which read as arrows striking the ground at varying inclinations. This tilt of structure across the roof gives its surface a distinctive twist, and a corresponding variation in the stance of the red supporting posts. The shifting section makes for subtly changing conditions across the width of the facility: how the wind blows across it, how the sun falls on it and the changing proportions of the sheltered space itself.

Beneath the roof the accommodation boxes correspond in form to the main structural grid of the building. Holding toilets, storage and administration facilities, they fold about the roof structure so that it can be seen in its entirety. The six metre grid was derived from the configuration archers take in international competition, and its clear articulation in built form is intended to strike a unity between competitors and the building behind them. The grid also serves to divide the structure into discrete units, allowing for flex and settlement on the underlying fill, with adjusting mechanisms built into the steelwork to trim the roof as it pivots on its hinged connections.

The sense of a didactic role for the building, where the strategy and details have a clarity of purpose which becomes evident on reflection, extends throughout. The Sydney Olympics were floated on a raft of promises to provide buildings mindful of current environmental concerns and the archery centre provides perhaps the most earnest view of how this might be achieved. The entire structure acknowledges its impermanence, and has

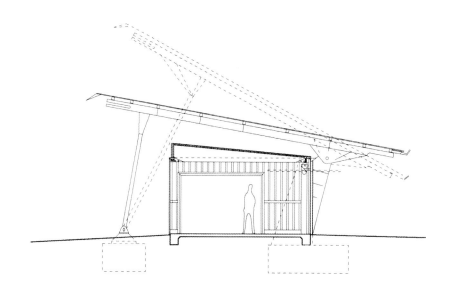

The Archery Centre consists of a pavilion made up of nine modular 'huts' set beneath a soaring skillion roof, lean and twisted to express not so much the literal flight of an arrow, as the whole idea of archery with its combination of power, grace and flight. The roof is anchored along the front edge by powerful concrete buttresses with expressed steel plate connectors from which the roof pivots using 75mm pins. The wave-like character of the roof derives from the varying sizes of the cantilevered plates. The structural self-assertion of the building expresses the independence of the roof and emphasises the tension between components. The result is a building whose poetry comes from its structure rather than its form and which functions as a metaphor for archery rather than a laboured representation of it.

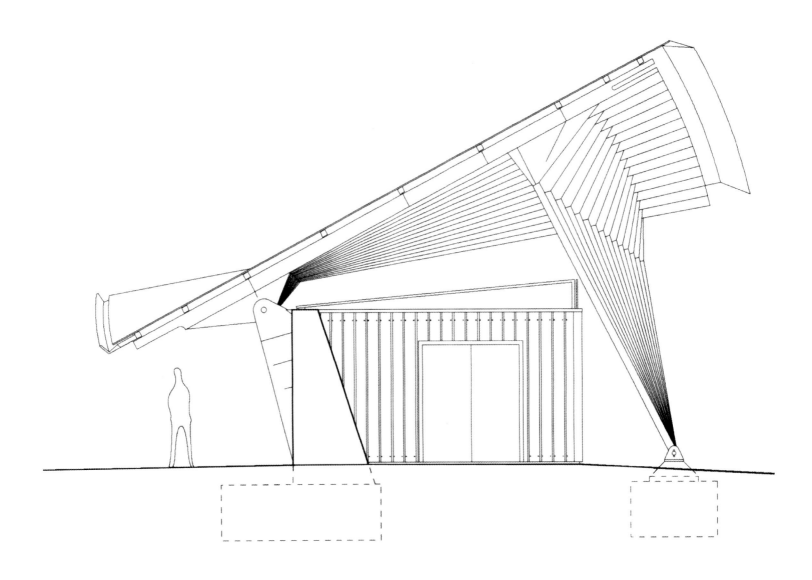

been designed to be reused elsewhere if disassembled. Timber members have been fixed top and bottom with this in mind. Metal sheeting remains in standard sizes, again allowing easy reuse. Fixings, too, have been considered, and much of the structure has been bolted together.

The demands of security have led to a system of polycarbonate rooflights shielded by mesh. This results in the boxes presenting mute faces when closed, with no visible windows. Internally, though, the even light has a carefully judged intensity. Within the toilets this washes over an array of meticulous, and sometimes ingenious details.

Considering the level of integrity with which the design of the archery centre was approached, the building could well stand for a cohesive vision of how a rational architecture, tempered by a sense of the poetic and careful in its use of resources, might look. The result, not unexpectedly, has a strong sense of handcraft with a finely-honed attendant feel for weight and size of components. It conveys the historical role of architecture as an argument, an embedded set of beliefs discernible in the layers of decisions which shape any building undertaken with the rigour of conviction. Perhaps the building's major failing is to misjudge its own permanence for didactic effect, given how comfortably it whistles in a light afternoon breeze. HARRY MARGALIT

Architect Bligh Voller Nield
Construction Abigroup
Engineering Ove Arup & Partners
Project Management NSW Department of Public Works and Services

NSW TENNIS CENTRE

The Sydney Olympic Tennis Centre is the visual climax of the south end of Olympic Boulevard. The circular high-tech roof of the centre court is aligned perfectly on axis and is one of the world's first circular centre court stadia. Adding to its urban qualities as termination to one of Homebush Bay's most important vistas, the circular plan (actually a 24 sided polygon) produces an intimate arena with excellent sightlines. Recessed into the earth, one enters at mid-level with seating tiers above and below for 11 000 spectators. With no requirement for a retractable roof, the stadium canopy is a lightweight steel structure with a supporting ring beam propped dramatically by angled steel struts. Precast concrete seating, galvanised steel and off-form concrete result in a clearly expressed saucer-like structure topped by a floating umbrella roof which provides shade for 70 per cent of spectators. As much of the stadium is below ground level, cooler air can be drawn from a basement tunnel and forced out by convection. Efficient air change will be stimulated by special grilles at the lower level as the stadium heats up in the summer sun.

Most visitors to the Tennis Centre will cross the three bridges over Boundary Creek and arrive in a garden environment with formal rows of Australian trees: Banksia, Illawarra flame trees, bottle-brush and tea-trees. The Centre is flanked by two show courts (4000 and 2500 spectator capacity), seven match and six practice courts, all surfaced in Rebound Ace. Together with an administration block and public facilities, all are laid out within an orthogonal pattern of tree-lined promenades. Venue for Olympic tennis and Paralympic wheelchair tennis, the Tennis Centre replaces Sydney's much loved White City. PHILIP GOAD

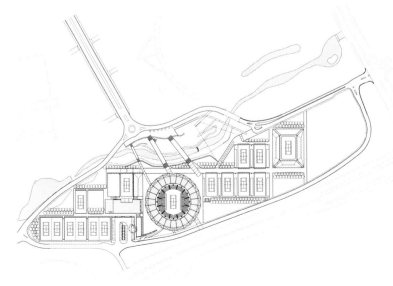

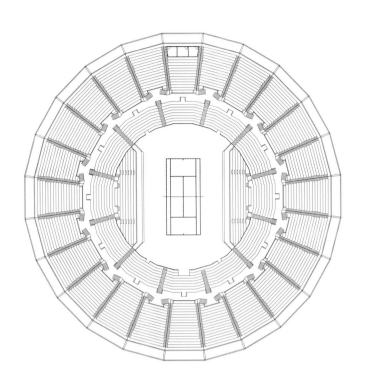

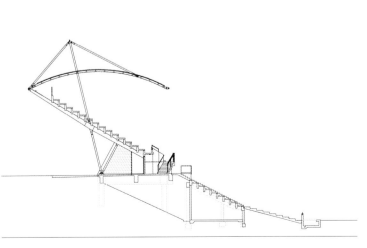

Architect Philip Cox Richardson Taylor and Peddle Thorp
Construction Civil & Civic (Lend Lease)
Engineering Connell Wagner
Project Management Civil & Civic

SYDNEY INTERNATIONAL AQUATIC CENTRE

S wimming has always been one of Australia's top performing Olympic sports. The XXVII Olympiad will be no exception, and all the nation's eyes will be focused on the Sydney International Aquatic Centre, which will receive a special temporary stand for the Olympic fortnight in expectation of huge crowds hoping to see records broken.

As one of the first venues to be completed at Homebush, the Aquatic Centre formed part of the master plan for the entire site, and its construction was an intrinsic element of Sydney's winning Olympic bid. The key masterplan concept was the creation of a distinct relationship between landscape and roofscape, and a series of stadia with the circle as their originating plan form. The aim, visually, was an expression of roof structure and either the submerging of arenas and grandstands into the landscape or the use of major landscaped berms against buildings to reduce their scale. This latter approach informed the design of the Aquatic Centre.

On arrival, one is made aware of the landscape-inspired solution immediately. The main entrance is through a circular hole in a massive grassed earth berm. One moves therefore from the bright light of the forecourt to a dark tunnel-like entry before entering into an ethereal aquatic blue lightworld and the echoing interior of the pool halls. To the left is the competition hall with its diving pool and competition pool. Built as a column free volume with a delicate steel latticework trussed roof, this spectacular space has tiered grandstands to either side. A ripple shaped bulkhead overhead is the dividing line between the competition zone and the smaller volume of the centre's leisure zone. Housing the training pool (which can be covered by the world's largest moveable floor) and an informally planned area of play pools, spas, water slide, rapid river ride, and even a 'beach' with fountains, spray jets and spurting volcanoes, this recreational section has contributed to the extraordinary popularity of the Aquatic Centre ever since its construction. Further whimsical nuance has been added by the inclusion of copses of palm trees and Sydney artist Colin Lanceley's swirling underwater murals.

The Aquatic Centre's roofscape echoes the gentle undulations of the surrounding landscape, while inside these curved roof forms create softly scaled light filled volumes. Designed within an overall circular footprint, the western half of the circle contains a landscaped garden with sinuous bands of coloured paving; another thematic reference to the early masterplan. The eastern semicircle contains the centre itself with its two articulated volumes: the larger volume, column free, contains the ten lane 50 metre competition pool and the 33 x 25 metre utility pool for water polo, diving and synchronised swimming; the smaller skylit volume contains the eight lane 50 metre training pool and all the recreational

AQUATIC CENTRE OLYMPIC EXPANSION
Architect Scott Carver
Construction Leighton Contractors
Engineering Connell Wagner
Project Management Sinclair Knight Merz

The beacon-like giant arched truss (above) which readily identifies the Aquatic Centre, is pivotal to the expansion of seating facilities in Olympic mode. The aerial photograph (opposite page) taken five years ago and before the straight Olympic Boulevard was built reveals the circular footprint on which the Aquatic Centre is based. The wave-like patterns are a feature of both the plan and elevation of the building and its landscaping. This is a strategy which partly echoes the gently undulating topography of the site and partly the idea of water. At the same time, by avoiding straight lines and sharp angles, the building achieves a feeling of human scale.

pools and associated spas, saunas, and steam rooms. Rising above these billowing forms, the overall silhouette of the centre is a white arched steel truss running the length of the complex. While it appears to hover above the landscape for no apparent purpose, it does have a very special function. It enables the giant earth berm which rests against the east wall to be removed, the arched truss then acting as a huge bridge-like beam. The eastern internal wall panels can then be taken away thus allowing a temporary stand to be inserted and an expansion of seating from 4400 to 15 000 spectators. Clad externally in plastic shrink-wrapped cardboard (a special product developed for this stand) and supported by dramatically angled struts, this new stand will have a striking effect. After the Games, the temporary stand is planned to be removed and re-erected elsewhere. This is fitting in an age of increasing concern for sustainable design and the possibility of large scale ephemeral structures being specially designed for major public events such as an Olympic Games. Besides this, the Aquatic Centre was always designed to be read as sitting within a park-like environment, not hard edged but humanly scaled and as one element amidst an entirely modelled landscape. PHILIP GOAD

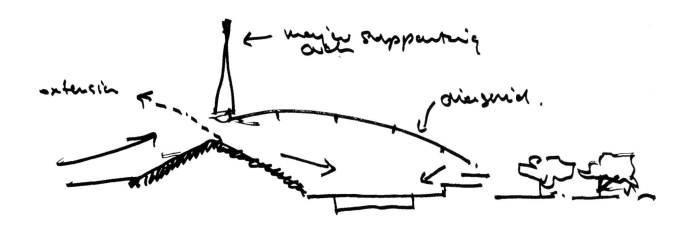

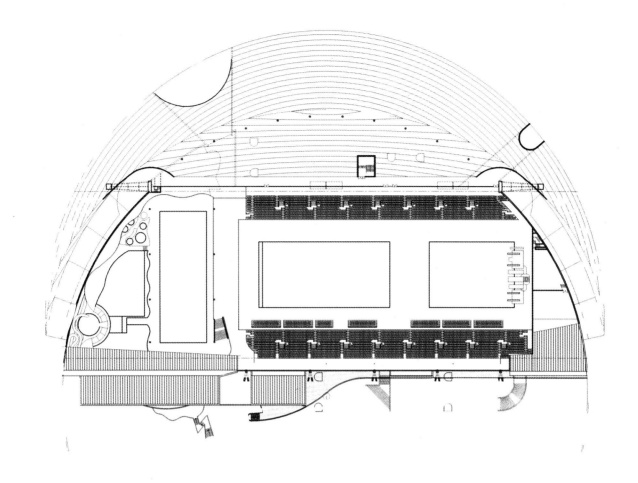

This view from beneath the diving boards shows
how wave forms are repeated inside the building.
Curved roof forms serve to soften the light inside
the Centre while a ripple-shaped bulkhead divides
the competition area from the popular leisure zone.

Like most of its contemporaries, the Sydney International Aquatic Centre is more than just a swimming pool, it is also an aquatic leisure centre with an area devoted to fun activities including spas, water slide, spray jets and an artificial beach. Also included is a free-form toddlers pool. Inspired while snorkelling off the Indonesian island of Lombok, architect Philip Cox asked the well-known Australian artist, Colin Lanceley, to design an underwater mosaic. Its imagery of eccentric sea creatures not only signals the happy informality of the Centre's leisure zone, but also acts as an easy contrast to the more utilitarian design and construction of the formal precincts elsewhere in the complex.

In order to allow additional temporary seating for the 2000 Olympic and Paralympic games it was necessary to increase the seating capacity from 12 000 to at least 15 000 without compromising the existing comfort and amenity levels. Since the temporary extensions face the Olympic Boulevard, it was also important to maintain the integrity of the existing building from this direction. The result, seen on this page, is a dramatic yet integrated extension to the Aquatic Centre which defies its temporary nature. Additional seating has been achieved mainly on the eastern stand, but with some additional seating on the western stand and a new stand on the gallery walkway bridge. The extension conforms with ESD principles by using largely recyclable building materials. It also allows for part of the structure to be retained as a post-Olympic legacy. The photographs on opposite page show the Aquatic Centre under construction in early 1994.

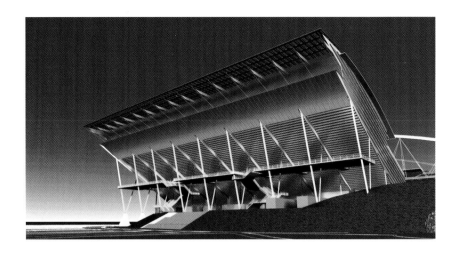

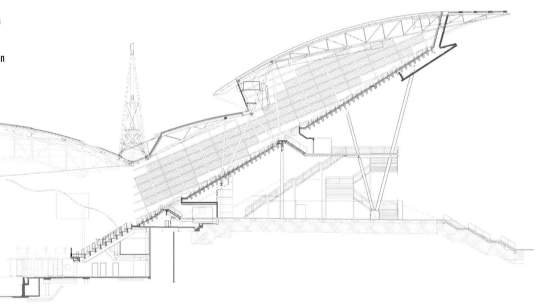

Developer Mirvac Lend Lease Village Consortium
Construction Civil & Civic
Engineering MPN Group
Project Management Mirvac/Lend Lease

OLYMPIC VILLAGE

The result of a design-construct bid from three development teams, the Olympic Village is located north across Haslams Creek on the site of a former munitions depot. The bid required that all housing be designed according to ecologically sustainable guidelines. Newington had to be 'green' and when complete, it will be the world's largest solar powered suburb. The village has four precincts: three housing and one commercial precinct comprising a retail complex, an eight hectare commercial and high-tech industrial zone, and a village green bordered by three storey apartment blocks. The housing areas contain double storey townhouses, courtyard houses, parks, and even a school. The master plan was later developed to include a band of medium rise apartments forming an urban wall facing south-east to the Homebush stadia thereby sheltering the suburb behind. The developer with its in-house team of architects collaborated with six architecture firms on the housing designs to ensure variety within a precinct that will eventually be home to more than 4500 people. There will be more than 2000 houses, townhouses and units. In Olympic mode, Newington will become an entirely different place with temporary dining halls, housing and recreational facilities and during the Games it will house 15 300 people.   PHILIP GOAD

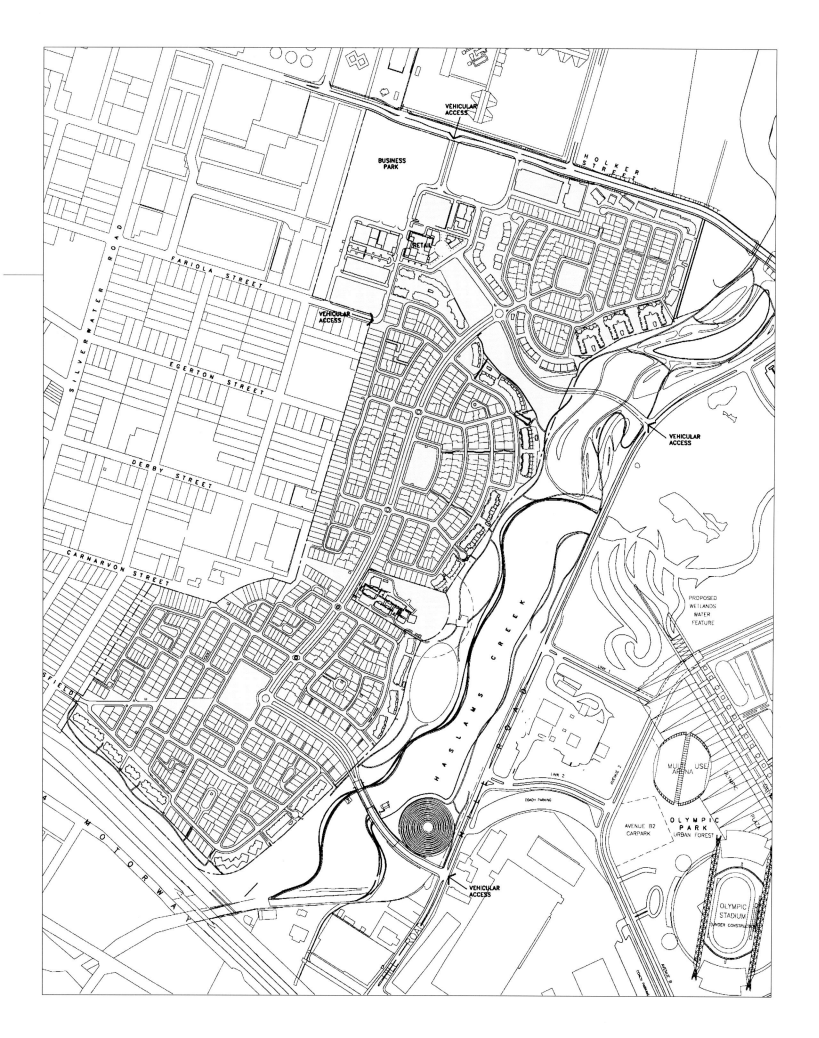

VEHICULAR
ACCESS

BUSINESS
PARK

H O L K E R
STREET

RETAIL

S I L V E R W A T E R   R O A D

FARIOLA   STREET

VEHICULAR
ACCESS

E G E R T O N   STREET

VEHICULAR
ACCESS

D E R B Y   STREET

C A R N A R V O N   STREET

PROPOSED
WETLANDS
WATER
FEATURE

SFIELD

H A S L A N S   C R E E K

LINK 1

LINK 2

AVENUE 2

MULTI USE
ARENA

M O T O R W A Y

R O A D

COACH PARKING

AVENUE B2
CARPARK

OLYMPIC
PARK
URBAN FOREST

VEHICULAR
ACCESS

OLYMPIC
STADIUM
UNDER CONSTRUCTION

COACH PARKING

AVENUE B

Architects HPA Architects, Bruce Eeles, Vote Associates
Construction Mirvac Construction
Engineering MPN Group

OLYMPIC VILLAGE
NEWINGTON APARTMENTS

The Newington apartments wind about the brow of a ridge, their sections stepping accordingly. From the east the profile recalls the most famous of their modernist predecessors, the interwar Weissenhof model development.

The apartments are unabashedly modernist in character, as evident in their planning, in the prevailing spatial sensibility within and in the composition and detailing which governs their appearance. They consist of two general types, a compact block with a compressed footprint and a U-shaped type with a stepped section and an internal court. Both are deft compositions, using the planes of the enclosing walls and roofs and a filigree of metal mullions and sunshading to provide the staggered volumes and play of light crucial to an effective modernist palette. All units open to the sun as far as possible, with many rooms having glazed, structure-free corners. Here the sunshading devices, a complex external layer both fixed and sliding, vertical and horizontal, play a crucial role in shielding these large glazed areas.

In the compact blocks the apartments generally span the depth of the building, with recessed terraces creating a fair measure of privacy. In the U-shaped blocks, a complex and ambitious configuration, the transparency demands a measure of idealism because of the limited privacy it affords. Yet for those holding a less guarded view of day to day living, the rewards are consistent with the higher promises of modernist architecture. The ground level apartments are contiguous with their landscaped surrounds, their large areas of glazing blurring the distinction between interior and exterior. The stepped section allows for several upper apartments with pavilion-like living areas and extensive terraces which luxuriously open to the sky. Each unit holds the promise of morning and afternoon sun.

The contrast between the apartments and the detached houses at Newington is a reminder of the ideals which sustain apartment living: convenience, security, outlook and the advantages of communal facilities and interaction. It is in the nature of apartments that these attributes vary with placement and planning, but at their best they project the experience of daily living well beyond the confines of the apartment walls. Indeed, for the topmost, all the way to the horizon. HARRY MARGALIT

The apartment buildings of Newington, two of
whose precincts make up the Athletes' Village,
stand almost emblematically across the ridge
overlooking the Olympic site. At the back they
form an urban edge to the detached houses which
complete the permanent residential area of this
new 'green suburb'. From the street, the
apartments are boldly white, but punctuated by
galvanised steel sunshades and saturated colours.
Combined with their heroically geometric forms
they represent an unambiguous acknowledgement
of the Modernist tradition of public housing. They
consist of two types. One type has a compressed
footprint with a limit of two apartments to each
landing. Here the apartments generally run the
full depth of the building optimising light
penetration and minimising energy requirements.

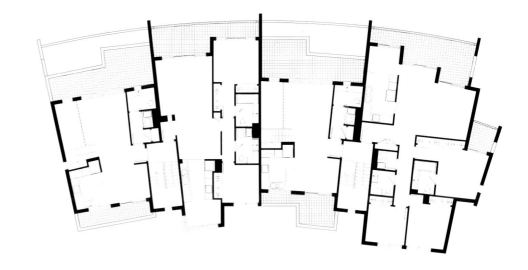

The U-shaped apartment blocks are stepped back against the fall of the ridge with terraced wings, a central courtyard and swimming pool. They offer a high degree of transparency to exploit the view to the Olympic venues, even as far as the skyline of the Sydney CBD, and to maximise light penetration to compensate for their generally south-easterly orientation. At ground level the apartments almost become a part of the gardens, while the upper apartments enjoy extensive terraces and pavilion-like living areas.

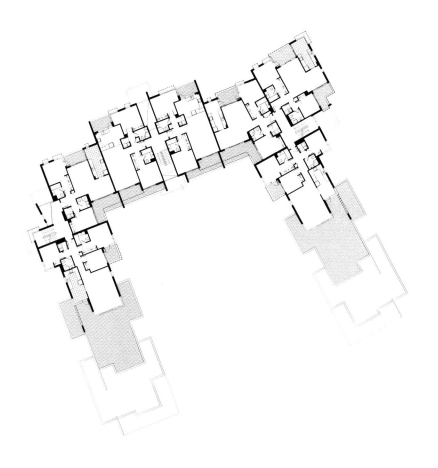

Developer Mirvac Lend Lease Village Consortium
Architects Virginia Kerridge, Grose Bradley,
Gordon & Valich, Order Architects,
Howard Tanner & Associates, Tonkin Zulaikha
Construction Mirvac Constructions
Engineering MPN Group
Project Management Mirvac/Lend Lease

OLYMPIC VILLAGE HOUSES

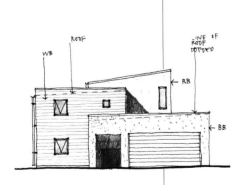

Three teams made up of pairs of young Sydney architects were invited to produce designs for the village's individual house types. Thematic ideas were workshopped and a select palette of materials, spatial and formal combinations were developed to provide a design formula of materials to relieve scale, provide textural interest and a mix of urban character. The development team and its architects then reworked all the suggested house types into a library of house plans for application to the site. Issues of streetscape, shade and private open space determined a village of zero lot lines grouped around a loose grid of streets and shared green spaces. All work within an orthodox set of material, spatial and physical parameters whilst following rigorous ecological sustainable guidelines. Four housing types were developed: family houses; courtyard houses; townhouses; and, for Olympic mode, portable accommodation pods. With the precincts planned to achieve a garden-like setting, the village housing will occupy just over one third of the 262 hectare site.

During the Games all the houses (other than those permanently occupied) will be without kitchen facilities and their interior spaces will be arranged to maximise the number of bedrooms. Over 900 temporary accommodation pods of two bedrooms and a bathroom will be dropped into courtyards and gardens as well as 500 relocatable homes. Garages will be converted to temporary bedrooms to accommodate four extra athletes per house. Finishes and materials will be minimal until after the Games when the houses will be re-fitted for private sale.

An important aspect of the Olympic Village is its proximity to the stadia – so different to many previous Games when athletes had to be transported considerable distances to sporting facilities. There is also another major point of significance. Newington has been privately developed and nearly all the houses and apartments will be sold before the Games begin. This project therefore has two aims: firstly, the provision of accommodation for the world's athletes and secondly, the successful development of a brand new ecologically sound suburb for Sydney. PHILIP GOAD

Architect Clare Design, Design Directors to the NSW Government Architect
Construction Abigroup
Engineering Department of Public Works & Services, Building Design Services
Project Management Department of Public Works & Services, Building Design Services

OLYMPIC VILLAGE SCHOOL

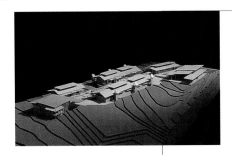

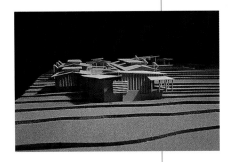

L ike most venues, the school has Olympics and post-Olympics functions. During the Games it will serve as a medical centre, and afterwards it will become a K-6 school serving the new suburb of Newington. Accordingly its design has been shaped by a mixture of considerations, such as the Environmentally Sustainable Design principles of the entire Olympic site, and the aesthetic of the surrounding suburban residential areas. Lindsay and Kerry Clare are renowned for their spirited and sophisticated buildings on the Sunshine Coast, north of Brisbane, which utilise lightweight materials to maximise ventilation and comfort. The logical and elegant simplicity of the Clares' approach to sub-tropical architecture has been adapted to suburban Sydney with this school. The long, lean skillion roofs incorporate a ventilated skylight system which creates internal spaces with improved air movement, temperature control, and balanced daylight. The pronounced timber tower structures for the solar panels give the buildings a distinctive profile as they step down a linear courtyard. This courtyard connects with large open spaces and smaller shaded areas to provide a variety of outdoor rooms for childrens' activities. Ramps integrated with the buildings and the landscape are the primary method of circulation. PAUL McGILLICK

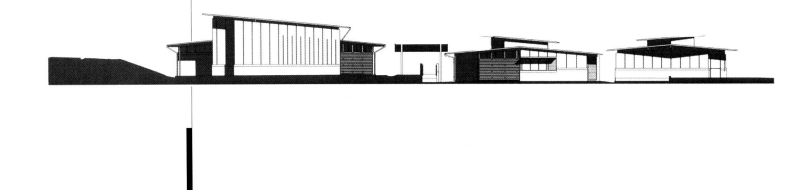

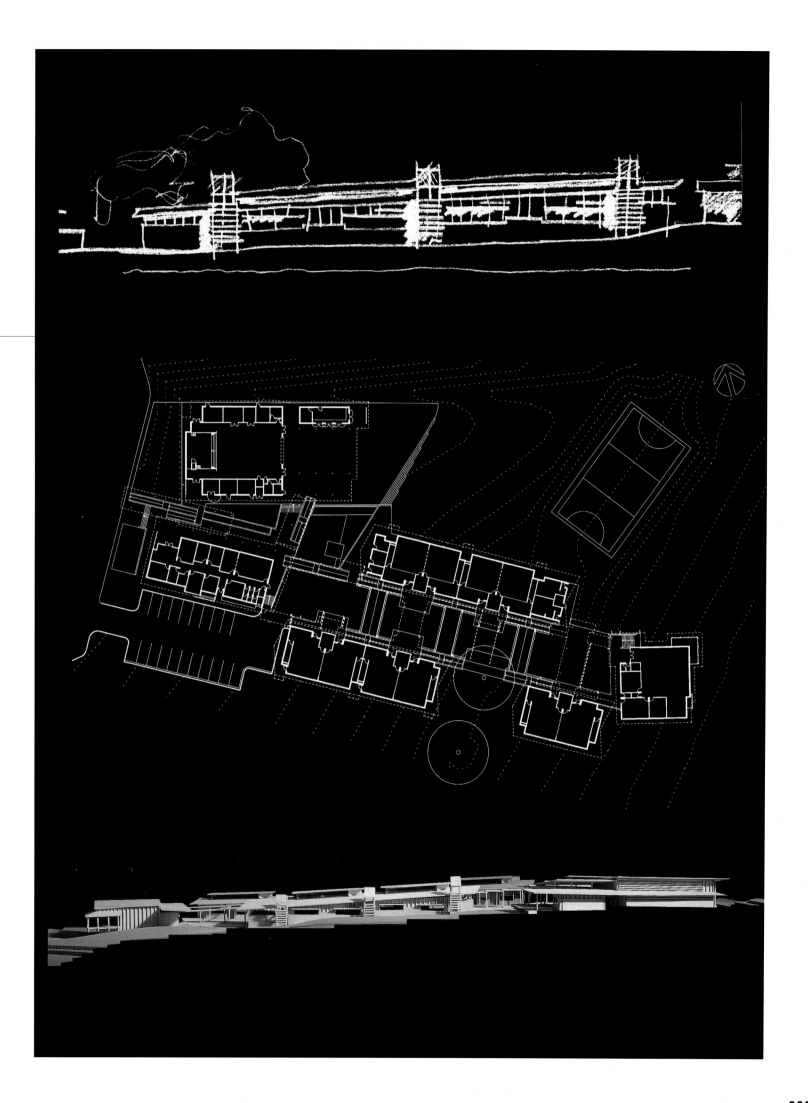

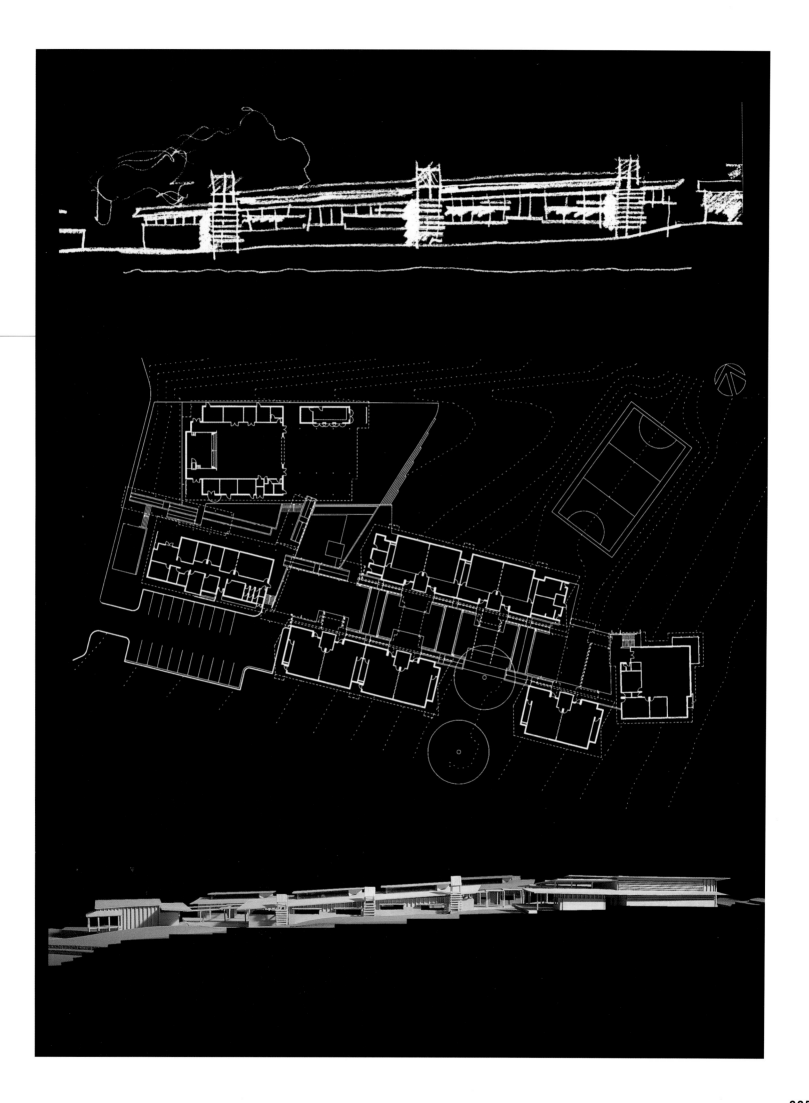

Architect Cox Richardson Architects & Planners in
association with Devine Deflon Yaeger
Construction Abigroup
Engineering Taylor Thomson Whitting

SYDNEY SUPERDOME

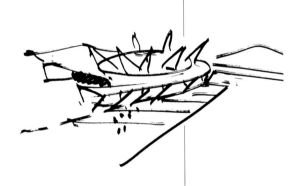

The enclosed counterpart of neighbouring Stadium Australia, the SuperDome is the country's largest indoor arena. Host to Olympic basketball and artistic gymnastics and Paralympic basketball, the SuperDome will continue as a privately operated venue for 30 years under an agreement between the Olympic Co-ordination Authority and the consortium responsible for its development and operation. Its event floor of over 3600m^2 has been sized with a wide array of sports, functions and productions in mind, and a retractable lowest tier of seats allows the seating capacity to be varied from 15 000 to 20 000. In all the seats rise through five levels, creating a towering ring of spectators with optimal sight lines and proximity to the action on the floor. The roof spans the space without the aid of internal columns, its mass stayed by cables tensioned over a series of perimeter strutting towers.

The arena is rendered more adaptable by its tight connection to adjacent facilities. A large hall feeds directly onto the event floor and an external service yard, each of which can be used separately or as an ensemble, where the hall might serve as a warm-up space for gymnastics or overflow space for a large trade exhibition. A car park with 3400 spaces abuts the complex, with direct access for club and corporate members. Further spill space is provided by a vast foyer which wraps around the northern side, allowing crowds to decompress as they make their way out into the northern part of the Olympic plaza which the SuperDome shares with the stadium.

The SuperDome incorporates a range of measures to decrease consumption of water and energy. These include systems for utilising stormwater and recycled water, air-conditioning which can be restricted to occupied portions of the building only, and a roof-mounted solar generating array which will feed up to 70 kW into the electricity grid.

Given that the Olympic site consists of reclaimed and remediated industrial sites and landfill, the major facilities were designed with few existing structures to limit their placement. The grouping of the various components which comprise the SuperDome and carpark is one attempt to create a cluster of buildings which varies the density of building across the Olympic site, rather than a series of isolated pieces with unimpeded access but little opportunity for the flexibility of use and accumulation of facilities which close proximity engenders. HARRY MARGALIT

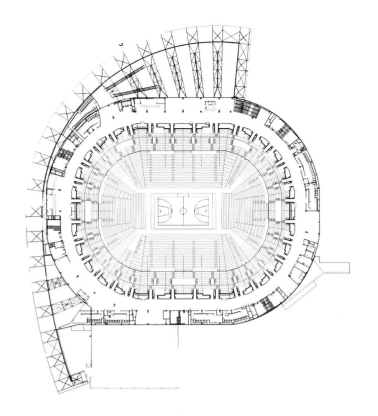

The SuperDome has been designed to cater for a wide array of sports, functions and productions. To facilitate this a retractable lowest tier of seats allows for the seating capacity to be varied from 15 000 to 20 000. As shown in the section (right), all of the seats rise through five levels, creating a towering ring of spectators with optimal sightlines and proximity to the action on the floor. The roof spans the internal space without the aid of internal columns and the mass is stayed by cables tensioned over a series of perimeter strutting towers.

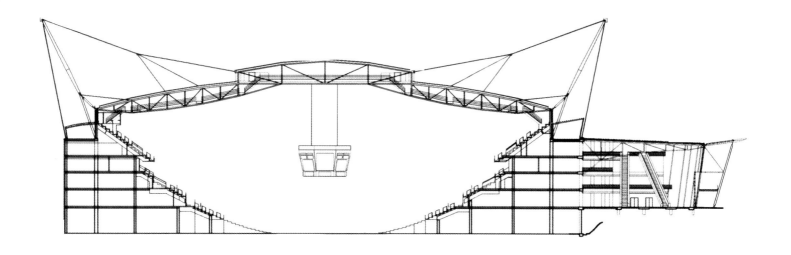

SYDNEY EXHIBITION CENTRE
& SYDNEY CONVENTION CENTRE,
DARLING HARBOUR

The redevelopment of Darling Harbour for Australia's Bicentennial in 1988 transformed a site of disused railway tracks, goods sheds and cargo wharves immediately to the west of the city. Olympic venue for Graeco-Roman and freestyle wrestling, boxing and judo, the Sydney Exhibition Centre comprises five interconnecting halls, and achieves a modest scale by virtue of a continuous cable and mast structure. Across the freeway to the north lies the more robust Sydney Convention Centre, which is the Olympic venue for weightlifting. Consisting in plan of a shell-like juxtaposition of two differently sized semi-circles, this monumental concrete edifice provides a contrast to the other more ethereal structures at Darling Harbour, though integrating logically with the adjacent freeway flyovers. A new building links these two Bicentennial landmarks with a more ephemeral translucent connection underneath the flyovers, and provides an alluring architectural sequence when lit at night. PHILIP GOAD

© Patrick Bingham-Hall and Haycraft Duloy

SYDNEY EXHIBITION CENTRE
Architect Philip Cox Richardson Taylor
Construction Leighton Contractors
Engineering Ove Arup & Partners
Project Management Darling Harbour Authority

SYDNEY CONVENTION CENTRE
Architect John Andrews International
Construction Baulderstone
Engineering Miller Milston and Ferris
Project Management Leighton Contractors

CONVENTION CENTRE SOUTH
Architect Ancher Mortlock Woolley
Construction NSW Department of
Public Works and Services
Engineering Connell Wagner
Project Management NSW Department of
Public Works and Services

Architect Philip Cox Richardson Taylor
Construction Civil & Civic
Engineering Ove Arup & Partners
Project Management Civil & Civic

SYDNEY FOOTBALL STADIUM, MOORE PARK

L ocated in Moore Park, inner Sydney, the existing Sydney Football Stadium is the venue for Olympic football (soccer). Completed in 1988 as part of Australia's bicentennial celebrations, the 40 000 seat stadium has a spectacular sweeping silhouette – the result of the demands of a rectangular playing field within an overall perimeter circular footprint. It further satisfies the need to maximise seating capacity across the middle of the field for optimum sightlines and has resulted in a dramatic signature structure. The canopy, designed to cover 25 000 spectators, is composed of white painted tubular steel which is repeated around the stadium perimeter. Outside, the soaring upper edge of the stadium has infills of taut windbreaking fabric whilst inside, the line of the canopy determined by the rise and fall of the seating creates a dynamic fluid line, providing an atmospheric sporting theatre. PHILIP GOAD

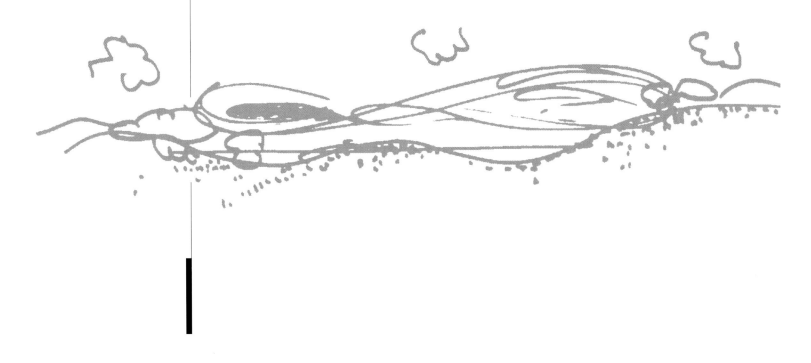

Architect Scott Carver
Construction St Hilliers
Engineering Patterson Britton & Partners
Project Management Australian Pacific Projects

OLYMPIC SAILING SHORE BASE, RUSHCUTTERS BAY

For the first time in the history of the Olympic Games, the sailing events will be held in the host city itself – because Sydney Harbour offers the ideal venue. The shore base for the sailing events is in Rushcutters Bay, and caters for all the behind-the-scenes needs of the competition. Here the very first naval building in Sydney (it was moved to this site from Bennelong Point early in the century) has been restored to serve as the base with a lift inserted to make the upper levels of the building accessible. A temporary marina for all the service vessels has been constructed from a series of floating pontoons up to 300 metres long (to be sold off after the Games) together with storage areas for the competition vessels. Environmentally Sustainable Design principles have been adhered to throughout and include water management and run-off control, natural lighting and thermal comfort of buildings. The adjacent park has also been upgraded (although the site itself will not be a spectator venue) which will become a valuable amenity for local residents. PAUL McGILLICK

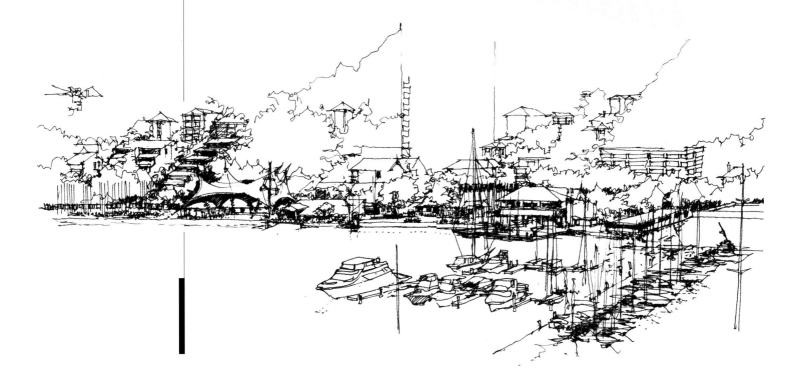

Architect Michael Davies Associates
Construction Haskins Contractors
Engineering Sinclair Knight Merz
Project Management Incoll Management

OLYMPIC SOFTBALL SPORTING FACILITIES, BLACKTOWN

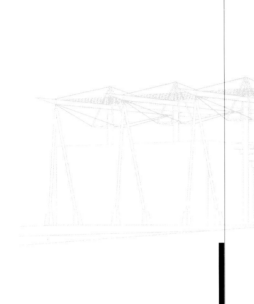

Master planning and design of the Aquilina Reserve in Blacktown took into account that, post-Olympics, the facilities would be available for community use including softball, baseball and athletics facilities. Hence, the need to balance the formality of the site as an Olympics venue and State sports centre with its regional setting, especially the bushland context. Given the rich wetland ecology and the adjacent Nurrangingy Reserve, it was decided to keep a bushland feel to the venue rather than that of a more formalised sporting venue. The State Softball Centre provides three diamonds for the Olympics, and a fourth for post-Olympics use. The four fields are aligned in a 'wagon wheel' configuration with the main competition diamond taking the optimum south-easterly orientation. The stadium consists of three levels with player amenities, offices for Softball NSW and boardroom and scorer positions on the top level. Seating 1000 people, it is covered by an elegant, but dramatic, cantilevered steel framed roof. The stadium integrates with the landscape with its lowest level concealed within an earth mound. PAUL McGILLICK

Architect Peddle Thorp & Walker and Donovan Payne Architects Joint Venture
Construction John Holland Construction and Engineering
Engineering Hughes Trueman Reinhold
Project Management Australian Pacific Projects

RYDE AQUATIC LEISURE CENTRE

The qualifying matches in the water polo competition will be held at the Ryde Aquatic Centre with the finals being held at Homebush Bay. The facility being built here replaces the previous centre which had deteriorated with age. Hence, the primary purpose of the project is to create a facility for the Ryde community and the Olympics overlay will be removed after the Games. It is a fully enclosed community facility consisting of a lightweight steel frame structure with modular façade and glazing system. The building is very transparent, so that people relaxing on the lawns outside can see through to the southerly aspect and out towards Parramatta River in the distance. The pool is designed to control sun glare as a safety feature. The building works on two levels on a sloping site. The upper level, accessed from the main entry at street level, offers a dry sports hall with seating for 200 people. The water sports facilities on the lower level include a competition pool, a programme pool (for disabled and rehabilitation use, and swimming classes) and a leisure pool with slides, whirlpool, river ride, toddlers' pool and zero beach. The competition pool provides seating for 4000 people which will reduce to 400 after the Games. PAUL McGILLICK

Architect Travis McEwen Group

Construction Civil & Civic

Engineering Connell Wagner

Project Management Lend Lease Projects

HOMEBUSH BAY HOTEL

The Homebush Bay Hotel is the tallest building on the Olympic site and, as such, is an important orientation point, marking the intersection of Dawn Fraser Avenue and Olympic Boulevard at the Yulang. A 70 metre spire on the north side of the tower creates a vertical reference point for the site. The smooth, modern, curvilinear shape of the main tower reflects the forms of the surrounding sporting venues.

The Homebush Bay Hotel actually consists of two hotels back-to-back, sharing combined back-of-house facilities. There are 150 3-star Ibis rooms and 168 4-star Novotel rooms. The elliptical plan of the Novotel tower has its long axis aligned with Olympic Boulevard and is flanked by the simple cubic forms of the Ibis hotel to the south and the function facilities to the east. The restaurants, bars and function rooms take advantage of the views to Stadium Australia and create an active edge to the Yulang.

Energy conservation features of the complex include one of Australia's largest commercial solar hot water systems, a 40% reduction in energy consumption, waste minimisation and naturally ventilated guest rooms with automated air conditioning which operates only when the windows are closed. PAUL McGILLICK

© Janet Laurence 1998

PUBLIC ART

BRIDGET SMYTH

The Sydney 2000 Olympic Games may be considered as a 'theatre of inquiry', whereby the architecture, art and urban design speaks for our aspirations in specific ways. One part of this inquiry is the special program incorporating the works and ideas of contemporary artists into the infrastructure and facilities necessary for hosting the Games. In Australia there has been no other project of such scale and significance, aside from Parliament House, that integrates art with architecture and urban design. The result for the Sydney Olympics is not a simple public gallery of outdoor art works but a built environment invigorated by artistic vision, and a cultural legacy beyond the Games. The public art program is an important initiative because, while there are many international examples of urban projects involving artists, it is something rare in Australia.

In the past twenty years there have been two main approaches to public art. Either sculpture is placed in an open air museum environment, such as Barcelona's public space program of the 1980s, or artists are included as design team members along with architects, landscape architects or urban designers, which happened with the St Louis Metro system and Phoenix Public Works program in the United States. For Sydney's Olympic Games, the second model has been adopted, whereby artists work alongside architects and urban designers to create public art that is contextually grounded and responsive to the overall design aspirations of the site at Homebush Bay.

While art may seem a long way from sport, there is a history of art being associated with the Olympic Games. The Olympic Charter is not dedicated to sport alone: it also embodies a commitment to the environment and to culture. In recent times the focus of that commitment has been on the environment, but in Sydney the focus is being re-balanced with a corresponding commitment made to art. Until 1948, the International Olympic Committee actually gave awards for art, a reflection of the classical Olympic ideal of the integration of mind, body and spirit.

Beyond the desire to recover this venerable Olympic principle, there is a desire to integrate public art in the built environment in order to enhance the Olympic site. The physical presence of art works that engage eyes, ears and minds, in fact whole bodily perceptions, provides a pleasurable layer of discovery and inquiry to people's experience of the Homebush site. The ideas behind the art works can be enjoyed and understood at many levels, from the purely experiential pleasures of visual and tactile contact to a more cerebral appreciation of their art. The works serve important civic and urban functions by marking significant sites. They also help define specific places, thereby making it easier for people to comprehend the site and orient themselves. Additionally, the artworks animate and transform the public spaces around buildings and express civic pride. They give identity to the Olympic site.

The Olympic Co-ordination Authority's Public Art Strategy initially developed a masterplan to determine where artists could make an impact on the public spaces of Homebush Bay. Next, the processes were put in place to ensure that artists' visions would be realised amidst the vastness of the construction process. A Public Art Advisory Committee (PAAC) was established and a team of public art professionals formed within the Olympic Co-ordination Authority's Urban Design Group. The ensuing development of public art projects took place within three clear stages: firstly, research into the site and the consolidation of project briefs; secondly, the shortlisting of artists by the PAAC, incorporating briefings and site visits with artists; and thirdly, the presentation of artists' concept proposals to the PAAC, collaborating designers and stakeholders, and the selection of a final artist to undertake the commission. Following this the commissioned artists began developing designs, collaborating with project designers and building contractors.

PUBLIC ART SITES

1 In the Shadow
2 Osmosis
3 Relay
4 5000 Calls
5 Overflow
6 Luminous Thresholds
7 Feathers and Skies
8 Discobolus
9 Lost and Found

PUBLIC ART

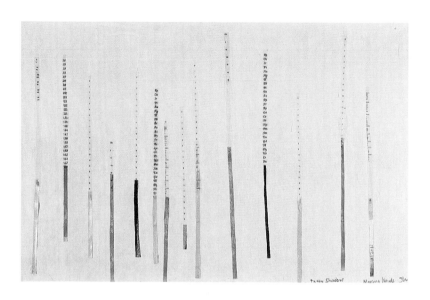

In the Shadow

IN THE SHADOW

Janet Laurence
Southern Terminus of Olympic Boulevard, Homebush Bay

The Southern Terminus of Olympic Boulevard posed an interesting contextual challenge: the task was to terminate the axis of the 1.6km Olympic Boulevard, reinforce the links to the International Tennis Centre, and respond to the immediate landscape of Boundary Creek.

The artist has avoided the strategy of an axial monumental object terminating the grand Boulevard, and instead reinforced the natural seclusion of the existing creek that provides such a sharp contrast to the large architectural spaces. *In the Shadow* is an environmental artwork that uses the movement of pedestrians across three bridges to the 14 000 seat Tennis Centre, and reflects on the processes of the natural environment.

An ensemble of disparate elements, fog, wands, and casuarinas is choreographed. Twenty-one tall vertical and transparent wands stand at various heights in Boundary Creek and conceptually measure chemicals and other substances monitored regularly in the water system. Atmospheric fog rises and dissipates, transforming and cooling the creek environment. The edges of the creek are lined with bullrushes, and a casuarina forest on either side frames the work and creates a soft green ribbon-like passage against the robust urban forms of the Tennis Centre and the Boulevard. Aerated water blurps randomly, drawing people directly into the intimate space of the creek laboratory.

'The work aims to reveal the transforming chemistry of remediation by creating a poetic alchemical zone as a metaphor for the actual transformation of Homebush Bay from its degraded contaminated industrial past into a green and living site for the future.'

Through revealing the invisible processes of Boundary Creek's water system, Janet Laurence creates a moment of intimacy and quiet amidst the passing crowd.

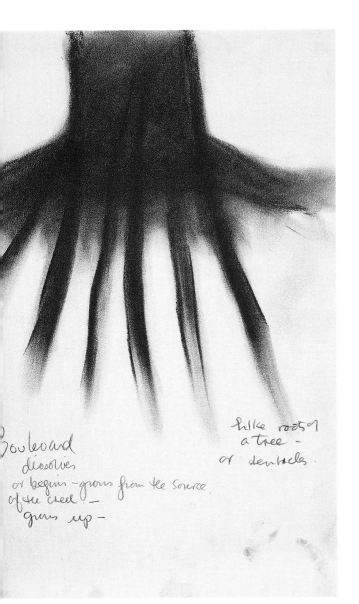

Boulevard
dissolves
or begins — grows from the source
of the creek —
grows up —

like roots of
a tree —
or dentacles.

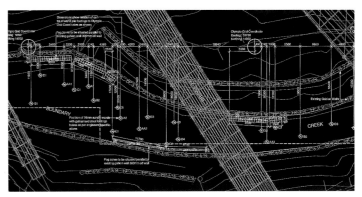

PUBLIC ART

OSMOSIS

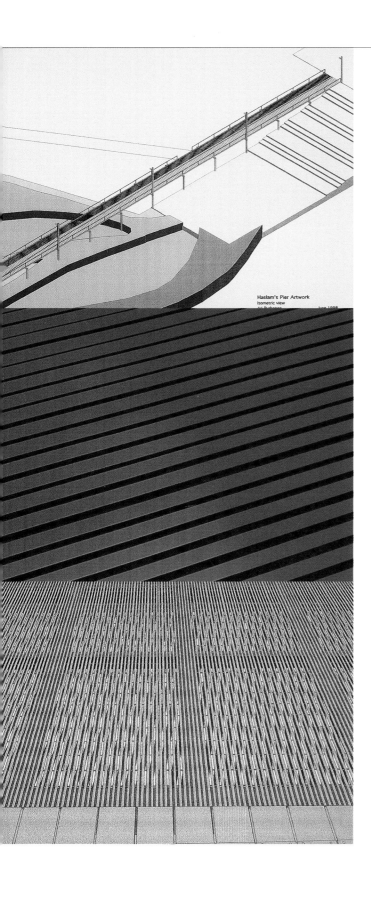

Haslam's Pier Artwork
Isometric view
Ari Purhonen

Ari Purhonen
Haslams Pier, Northern Water Feature, Homebush Bay

The Northern Water Feature, designed by Hargreaves Associates, is an enormous earthwork that transforms landfill and run-off water into a sculpted artificial landscape. It provides a critical transition zone between the urban core sporting and recreational facilities, and the threshold to the Millennium Parklands.

The brief was to work with the 112m long Haslams Pier, which is like a wharf where one can watch endlessly the passing and movement of water and the wildlife beneath.

Ari Purhonen developed an artwork that acts as a visual filter between the human body and the underwater environment. 'Purification occurs beneath the surface in a silent and magical way. Processes of assimilation, osmosis, photosynthesis and evaporation occurring in the wetlands are invisible to the human eye. The pier floats lightly and elegantly over the wetlands. Pedestrians flow from the boulevard horizontally over the water feature and out over the treatment ponds.'

Eight metres below the pier, a series of wetland ponds captures run-off water from Olympic Boulevard and cleanses it through aeration and sunlight, and through settlement and filtration by plant life.

This artwork acts as an intervention into the pier structure in two layers. A thin metal inlay into the recycled hardwood planking aligns with the axis of the boulevard to the south and curves gently away from the built edge of the site, gesturing towards the parklands beyond. The second intervention is a colourful ladder-like series of forty-five grid panels sitting beneath the open web-forge pier floor. The grid panels make reference to the shifting grid of the Olympic Plaza paving pattern, yet each panel shifts its grid, creating a dynamic visual effect when viewed through the web-forge. The angle of the artwork grid begins in the south with a ten degree offset and shifts one degree every ten metres until the last panel is parallel with the web-forge grid. This creates greater transparency as one moves along the pier, with the environment below unfolding with dramatic rainbow shifts in colour. 'The colours of the grid are taken from the visible spectrum of light, echoing the rainbows created by the Water Feature when seen against the sun.'

PUBLIC ART

All photography © Patrick Bingham-Hall

Drawings © Paul Carter and Ruark Lewis, and OCA

TEXT SCROLL 4

Tier E16.3 ~ E20.3

BUTOUTOFDEPTHSWATERMOTIONINGSTONETOCRADLEMOVINGFORMSPLUNGESHADOWSHAPETH
SEMIMONSTERSOSWIFTANDBLITHESOMEWATERBORNEADROITASDIVERSHEAROHERAOURBLOOI
STARTLELOVELYLIONOFATHENEVERFALLBEATENOTIMETOPUFFRESHLYOUSONOFSTONEAROART
NOVICTOREARNOWALKNOTMARCHCOURAGENDURESLOVESHALLOFAMEANDOINARYWONDERSPO
WEARELIKETHEDARKSIDEOFTHEMOONTHEREBUTSOLITTLEKNOWN

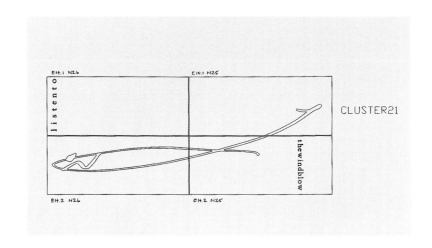

RELAY

Paul Carter and Ruark Lewis
Fig Grove, Homebush Bay

The Fig Grove is on the edge of Olympic Plaza, a central refuge formed by ten mature fig trees which once provided shade to the former abattoir.

Visual artists and writers were asked to compose a text for this major public space to reflect on the Australian experience of the Olympic Games. Artists Paul Carter and Ruark Lewis developed a text consisting of two layers: 3000 letters sandblasted into the vertical surfaces of one kilometre of granite seating risers, and thirty 'graffiti clusters' strewn across the horizontal seating surfaces.

'*Relay* is not a monument but a celebration of memorial, fleeting instances. The words composing the texts share their first and last letters, as if a baton is being handed on from one word to the next. To read the text is like watching a race - the polychromatic design, revealing hidden words inside words, creates the similitude of runners jockeying for position. *Relay* is about ordinary moments transfixed in memory; and as different words jostle for attention, it is as if the different experiences of each of us are being represented.'

Each of the four tiers of seating represents an era of the modern Olympic Movement. The red tier represents the 1896 inaugural games; the yellow tier is for the 1956 Melbourne Olympics, the golden years of post-war prosperity; the blue tier stands for the Sydney 2000 Olympics, the millennial games in the harbour city; and the green tier projects beyond 2000 to aspirations for a balanced coexistence with the natural environment. With the generous assistance of Harry Gordon, Olympic historian, the graffiti clusters reveal the often playful and irreverent handwriting of some of our most renowned Olympians.

This artwork transforms the Fig Grove into a special place where Australia's sporting histories are woven through time in the written word. 'The sleek, clear lines of steps which Hargreaves designed are slightly tilted. Taking advantage of this, *Relay*'s lower lines gradually slide into the ground, then they resurface; and the lyrical messages which weave through the graffiti designs are continuations of the lines which have gone underground. In this way the text and architecture inform each other; and visitors, enjoying the fountains, the cool of the shade, the glittering walls and floors of text, are moved by the true Olympic Spirit.'

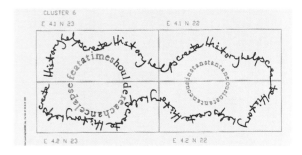

PUBLIC ART

5000 CALLS

David Chesworth and Sonia Leber
Urban Forest, Homebush Bay

Surrounding the monumental Stadium Australia is the 4.5 hectare Urban Forest, an expansive public space planted with a loose grid of hundreds of eucalyptus trees. The work transforms the experience of moving through this space of anticipation.

Sound artists David Chesworth and Sonia Leber conceived a sound environment composed wholly of human vocalisations: 5000 individual sounds of the human voice and breath, ranging from a weightlifter's grunt, to a labourer's breathing, and the chanting of monks. This collection of 5000 calls constitutes the largest permanent human soundscape to be used in an outdoor public space. With its ephemerality and dynamism, the art work stands in total contrast to the weighty monumentality of the Stadium.

Different sounds are projected into different zones by eighty speakers mounted discreetly on light fixtures throughout the forest. Motion sensors in the pavement gauge movement and trigger volume and composition changes. Only after five hours would one hear the same sequence of breaths and voices.

'Not able to hear the word, we hear the grain of the voice, the many grains of voices captured during performing various tasks, perhaps like the 'proto-linguistic' vocalisations which preceded language. We hear the body at work, the flow of air through the body tracing the shape of the throat; the vibrating qualities of the individual vocal chords; the shape and capacity of the body. We hear only fragments of voices: stressing, straining, singing, in laughter and in pain. We hear effort in the voice and breath; the body in work. These are direct, uncomplicated calls. Short and fast, they are meant to be immediately understood. They are combined here with the stretched out proclaiming voice of the singer, the priest and others. Sometimes a particular voice appears as if held in suspension. Captured and frozen like a photograph, it is as though the sound of that moment were held in time and we are able to walk through a particular body signature.'

It is difficult to convey in words the experiential quality of such works. Through minimal means, this artwork transforms the expansive space and infiltrates it with mood and evocation.

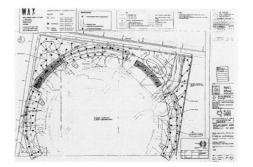

PUBLIC ART

Black and white photography © Patrick Bingham-Hall; all other images © Peter Cripps, Terri Bird, and OCA

Artist concept

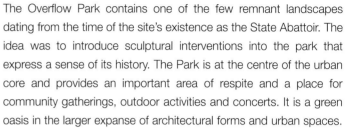

OVERFLOW

Peter Cripps and Terri Bird
Overflow Park, Homebush Bay

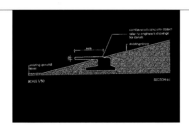

Artist prototype

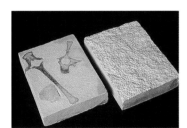

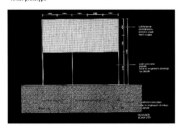

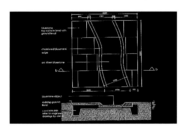

Artist concept

The Overflow Park contains one of the few remnant landscapes dating from the time of the site's existence as the State Abattoir. The idea was to introduce sculptural interventions into the park that express a sense of its history. The Park is at the centre of the urban core and provides an important area of respite and a place for community gatherings, outdoor activities and concerts. It is a green oasis in the larger expanse of architectural forms and urban spaces.

Artists Peter Cripps and Terri Bird have introduced a series of minimal sculptures that capture a reading of the site's past. Four artworks are located and scaled according to the artists' topographical analysis. The objects assume the site as a surface, with each object placed according to a precise datum point on an imaginary plane.

Four sculptural objects create an ensemble. *Buried Object 400* is a recessed form 4m below the park's surface: made of bluestone, this piece suggests the site's layered history. *Cantilevered Ground Object* is a 16m long form projecting into the air from beneath an avenue of trees; it registers the artificial earth forms of the park's new landscape. The cast concrete artwork has a revealed bone surface, a reference to the former abattoir. *Above Ground Object 4800* is 4.8m high and 6m long, made of perforated galvanised sheeting. It is sited in the avenue of trees and reframes this linear space; sedimentary layers record a layer of bones as the datum line. The slender vertical *Above Ground Object 2100* marks the datum through the transition of material layers. The lower layer is cast concrete with a revealed bone textured surface.

'These objects have been developed in response to the history of the site as a slaughter yard through the metaphor of embedding and layering material remnants. The work comprises a series of integrated objects that have been refined to engage with the avenue of trees as a primary site reference. The contour line of rl 113.6 has been chosen as it is the mid-way point between the higher and lower levels of the park. The 113.6 above rl operates as an imaginary plane connecting all objects through a datum line which sits above and below the gound's surface. The manner by which each object marks the datum level activates a relation between the topographical reading of the park's surface, associations with natural history and the layering formations of rocks through sedimentation. This extended reading of landscape affords a poetic discourse that allows a reading of history which coalesces in a spatial awareness of place.'

Cripps and Bird's archaeological reading of Overflow Park allows both an open, uncomplicated interpretation and, for those who seek a deeper reading, a rich interpretation of the past. The minimal and refined objects provide places to sit and lean against as well as a new layer of the site through which one can contemplate the past.

PUBLIC ART

Above photograph © Patrick Bingham-Hall; alll other images © James Carpenter and OCA

Artist concept, Southern Threshold

LUMINOUS THRESHOLDS

James Carpenter
Thresholds to Homebush Bay at Haslams Bridge and
Australia Avenue

Haslams Bridge site of Northern Threshold

James Carpenter with prototype

As a site of international significance, the arrival points to Homebush Bay were always intended to be marked in special ways, in particular the vehicular approaches from the north and south.

James Carpenter's *Luminous Thresholds* announce these gateways with dramatic and ethereal works that evoke a sense of the site's connection to water. To the north, at the Haslams Bridge gateway, a series of 30m high masts creates light paintings in the sky with sophisticated misting and natural and artificial light effects. During the day, a 30m mast housing a gigantic heliostat (mirror) captures daylight and redirects it through the misting devices. At night, artificial light is beamed through the mist. Drawing the eye beyond the immediate roadway environment, the work makes a connection to the broader creek and park landscape, where nature constantly transforms light and water in a dynamic cycle.

To the south at Australia Avenue, masts run parallel with the road, Bicentennial Park and the sculpted edge of the Homebush Bay core area. Visitors arriving at the site pass through an evanescent mirage of mist and colour.

'*Luminous Thresholds* focuses on the ordering nature of light, wind and mist. This emphasis on cycles in nature announces and articulates the masterplanning strategies of the Homebush Bay site. It explores the physical laws of the atmosphere by using a sequence of masts, dispersing a fine cloud of mist into the air. Through the reflected light from the heliostat, the sun's rays redirect light onto a drifting scrim creating a mirage effect. The demonic qualities of the atmosphere will engage pedestrians and vehicular passengers in the various optical phenomena such as sky brightness, colour rendition, haloes and rainbows. The threshold becomes a choreography of motion and time.' James Carpenter's poetic deployment of mist and light lifts the spirits and signals a place of sensitive engagement with the natural environment.

Artist concept, Northern Threshold

PUBLIC ART

DISCOBOLUS

Robert Owen
Stockroute Park, Homebush Bay

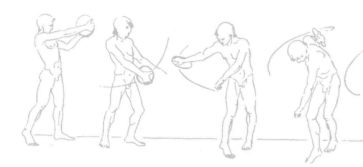

With a similar tribute constructed for the 1996 Atlanta Olympics, the Australian Hellenic Education Progressive Association proposed a tribute to the Australian Greek community for the Sydney 2000 Olympic Games in the hope that there will be a trilogy when the 2004 Games take place in Athens.

Stockroute Park at Homebush Bay is next to Olympic Park Station. It is a small, quiet, intimate place. Robert Owen's Discobolus pays homage to the origins of the Olympic Games and transforms Stockroute Park into a landscape of past and present.

The artwork has three components. A sacred olive grove with cypress trees refers to the trees planted in the original Olympic precinct. The Discobolus, one of the surviving pieces of sports equipment from the Grecian Games, has been transformed over time into the contemporary discus. Fragments of architectural details make reference to the ancient Olympian sites.

'The sculpture is based on the allegorical metaphor of Castor (son of Zeus), the original discus thrower, who metaphorically throws the disc from Greece to Homebush Bay. It has travelled through the millennia and lands, wedged into the ground, transformed into a huge 7m diameter metal disc symbolising a contemporary disc, the CD ROM, which refers to modern technology, information and culture.'

Discobolus is seen against the backdrop of monumental contemporary architecture, providing a constant reminder of the origins of the Olympic movement and the impetus for the creation of Homebush Bay.

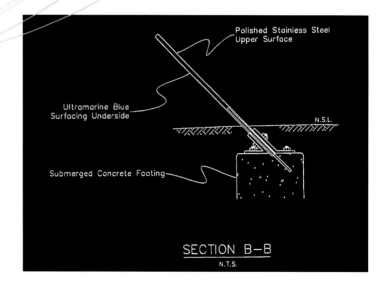

Photograph © Patrick Bingham-Hall; alll other images © Robert Owen and OCA

FEATHERS AND SKIES

Neil Dawson
Stadium Australia, Homebush Bay

Neil Dawson's *Feathers and Skies* marks arrival into Stadium Australia. Suspended beneath the arrival forecourt on both the eastern and western entries, the 22m diameter ellipses echo the victory wreaths adorning the building. The wreath to the east remembers local birds with abstracted feathers in finely cut, brightly coloured steel. The wreath to the west reflects the sky, with its clouds and ever-changing movement and colours.

Feathers and Skies is monumentally-scaled for the monumental building. The work engages with the architecture and transforms its grand face with gestures that provoke, surprise and awe.

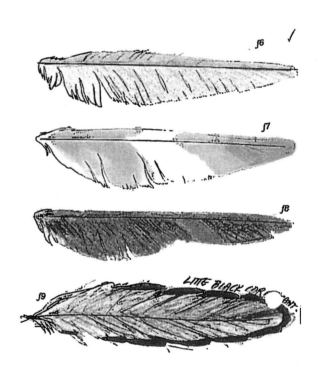

PUBLIC ART

© Patrick Bingham-Hall

LOST AND FOUND

Elizabeth Gower
Sydney SuperDome, Homebush Bay

The transparent SuperDome, with its large interior space, warranted a highly patterned floor. Elizabeth Gower's floor patterns celebrate the scale of the space and provide an appropriate underlay for the changing activities of this multi-purpose arena.

INTERNATIONAL SHOOTING CENTRE

One of Sydney's western Olympic Games' venues is also host to a public art project. The indigenous owners of the site, represented by the Gandangara Land Council, will collaborate with an artist to address the entry experience into this place and incorporate significant artefacts preserved by the Gandangara people.

MILLENNIUM PARKLANDS

The Millennium Parklands is the most expansive urban park created in metropolitan Sydney. It is a place of diverse landscapes, from pristine native habitats to remediated sculptural markers, and hosts a laboratory of the environment within its 450 hectares. A long-term vision of the park as the location for distinctive sculptural works is being developed.

SUMMARY

In reviewing this ambitious Olympic Public Art program, it is important to acknowledge the scale and diverse circumstances of Homebush Bay. Unlike other urban sites, Homebush Bay has no sense of containment. It is an unusual place that elicits grand gestures and absorbs the large-scale buildings, the diverse range of uses, and the huge transitory throngs of people that come and go. The landscape is expansive and often appears to have no edges or boundaries, except for the flaming evening skies. To introduce intimacy here is a challenge. The artworks in different and subtle ways reflect the scale and dynamism of the site, and articulate various experiential approaches.

The inclusion of public art as part of the Olympic site was based on the notion of public space as a theatre of inquiry; promoting curiosity, investigation, and even daring. This public art program sees public space as a democratic realm where the voices of artists may be heard. Given the complex nature of shaping public space, public art is an added and much needed evocation of cultural values.

'Lost and Found', SuperDome foyer

DESIGN & CONSTRUCTION LISTINGS

STADIUM AUSTRALIA

Development Manager: Olympic Co-ordination Authority

Architect: Bligh Lobb Sports Architecture

Structural Engineer: Modus Consulting Engineers and Sinclair Knight Mertz

Acoustic Engineer: Robert Fitzell Acoustics

Fire Engineer: Stephen Grubits and Associates

Electrical Engineer: D Rudd and Partners

Mechanical Engineer: D Rudd and Partners

Information Technology Engineer: Flack and Kurtz

Civil and Hydraulic Engineer: Sinclair Knight Merz

Lighting Engineer: Lighting Design Partnership, Thorn Lighting

Landscape: Site Image Landscape Architects

Disability Access Consultant: Independent Living Centre

BCA Consultant: Stephen Grubits and Associates

Quantity Surveyor: WT Partnership Australia

Construction: Multiplex, Obayashi

CONSULTANTS:

Passive Ventilation: Brian Ford & Associates

Pitch and Arena Geotechnical: Coffey Partners International

Traffic: Colston Budd Hunt and Twiney

Legal Adviser: Dunhill Madden & Butler

Signage & Graphics: Emery Vincent Design

Environmental: Enproc

Surveyor: Frank M Mason

Moving Seat Stands: Herk Edwards

Development Application Adviser: Ingham Planning

Daylight Analysis: Insearch

Carpet Advisor: Jim Cooper and Associates

Environmental Advisor: Karla Bell and Associates

Local Industry Plan: NSW ISO

Pitch & Arena: RA Young & Associates

Quality: SGS Quality

Wind Studies: The University of Sydney

Building Certifier: Trevor Howse and Associates

Photovoltaic Analysis: Unisearch

Crowd Modelling: Vitch Liester

Main Contractor: Multiplex Constructions

SUB CONTRACTORS:

Siphonic Drainage: Armpower

Scaffolding: Boral/Rocom

Site Security: BRN Security Services

Site Offices: Campac

Earthworks: Daracon Group

Reinforced Concrete Structures: De Martin & Gasparini

Mechanical Services: Environ

Piling: Frankipile Australia

Blockwork: Fugen Holdings

Lifts: Honeywell

Workforce Accommodations: James Hardie Building Systems

Hydraulics: John R Keith

Cranes: Kanabrook Cranes

Electrical Services: Kennedy Taylor

Site Communications: King Communications

Escalators: Kone Elevators

Cranes: Lampson Australia

Temporary Electrical: N & G Electrics

Steel Roof Trusses: National Engineering

Precast: Rescrete

Cranes: Santo's

Polycarbonate Roofing to east and west stands: Sky Solutions

Reinforcement Supply: Smorgan ARC

Tree Relocation: The Tree Doctor

Fire services: Tyco International

Prestressing: VSL Prestressing

Paving: Sam the Paving Man

Roof: Skydome

Joinery: MA Coleman Joinery

Ceilings & Partitioning: Interline Interior Linings

Ceilings & Partitioning: Interfit

Kitchen: Curtin Queensland

Seating: Sebel Furniture

Flooring: General Flooring

PUBLIC DOMAIN:
OLYMPIC BOULEVARD, THE OVERFLOW, YULANG AQUATIC CENTRE FORECOURT, STATE SPORTS CENTRE FORECOURT

Development Manager: Olympic Co-ordination Authority

Master Concept Designers: GADD/Hargreaves Associates

Head Consultant: Denton Corker Marshall

Design Team: Richard Johnson, Adrian Pilton, Paul Geehan, Maria Rigoli, John Madry, Tracey Symons, Phil Black, David Cameron, Belinda Rollandson, Erin Hrouda

Civil Engineer: Maunsell McIntyre

Electrical Engineer: Barry Webb & Associates

Graphics/Signage: Emery Vincent Design

ESD: Eco Design Foundation

Quantity Surveyor: Page Kirkland Partnership

Project Management: Gutteridge Haskins & Davey

Construction: Concrete Constructions

SUB-CONTRACTORS

Design Landscaping: Sam the Paving Man

OLYMPIC PLAZA

Head Consultant: Denton Corker Marshall

Civil Engineer: Maunsell McIntyre

Electrical Engineer: Barry Webb & Associates

Graphics/Signage: Emery Vincent Design

ESD: Eco Design Foundation

Quantity Surveyor: Page Kirkland Partnership

Project Manager: Gutteridge Haskins & Davey

Contractors: Multiplex (Southern half of plaza), Abigroup - Millennium (Northern half of Plaza)

Sub-Contractors: Sam the Paving Man

OLYMPIC BOULEVARD BUS SHELTERS

Head Consultant: Denton Corker Marshall

Civil Engineer: Maunsell McIntyre

Electrical Engineer: Barry Webb & Associates

Graphics/Signage: Emery Vincent Design

Quantity Surveyor: Page Kirkland Partnership

Project Manager: Gutteridge Haskins & Davey

Contractors: Lahey Constructions

YULANG SHELTER

Head Consultant: Denton Corker Marshall

Civil Engineer: Maunsell McIntyre

Electrical Engineer: Barry Webb & Associates

Quantity Surveyor: Page Kirkland Partnership

Project Manager: Gutteridge Haskins & Davey

Contractors: Stoddart

SOUTHERN TERMINUS (INCLUDES BRIDGES)

Head Consultant: Denton Corker Marshall

Civil Engineer: Maunsell McIntyre

Electrical Engineer: Enginuity

Lighting Designers: Lighting Design Partnership

Quantity Surveyor: Page Kirkland Partnership

Project Management: NSW Department of Public Works and Services

Contractors: Abigroup

HILL ROAD CARPARK AMENITIES

Development Manager: Olympic Co-ordination Authority

Architect: Ancher Mortlock & Woolley

Project Director: Dale Swan, Ancher Mortlock & Woolley

Project Architect: Deanne Rose, Ancher Mortlock & Woolley

Specification Writer: Phil Aitken, Ancher Mortlock & Woolley

Design Manager: Tom Irga, Gutteridge Haskins & Davey

Project Leader & Landscape Architect: Tract Consultants

Project Director: George Gallagher, Tract Consultants

Project Landscape Architect: Matthew Easton, Tract Consultants

Structural Engineer: Maunsell McIntyre

Civil Engineer: Maunsell McIntyre

Mechanical & Hydraulic Engineer: Maunsell McIntyre

Lighting & Electrical Services: Barry Webb & Associates

Cost Planning: Davis Langdon & Beattie

Signage Design: Minale Tattersfield Bryce & Partners

Project Management: Gutteridge Haskins & Davey

Construction: Lahey Construction

LIGHTING PYLONS

Development Manager: Olympic Co-ordination Authority
Architect: Tonkin Zulaikha Architects
Project Team: Peter Tonkin, Neil Mackenzie, Ellen Woolley, Paul Rolfe, Alex Haw, Stephen Varady
Lighting Engineers: Barry Webb and Associates
Structural Engineers: Taylor Thomson Whitting
Signing Consultant: Emery Vincent Design
Concrete: Precast Concrete Pty
Steelwork: National Engineering
Reflectors: Sky Solutions
Solar Panels: BP Solar
Lighting Equipment: Energy Australia
Project Management: NSW Department of Public Works and Services
Construction: Multiplex (Stadium Australia Precinct works), Abigroup (SuperDome Precinct works)

AMENITIES BLOCKS - CORE AREA

Development Manager: Olympic Co-ordination Authority
Architect: Durbach Block Murcutt
Project Team: Neil Durbach, Camilla Block, Joe Grech, David Jaggers, Nick Murcutt, Lisa Levan
Structural Engineer: Ove Arup & Partners
Hydraulic Engineer: Acor Consulting
Electrical Engineer: Lincolne Scott
Landscape Architect: Durbach Block Murcutt
Passive Solar Consultant: Advanced Environmental Concepts
Quantity Surveyor: Page Kirkland Partnership
Disability Consulting: Morris Disability Consulting
Signage Consultant: Emery Vincent Design
Project Management: Gutteridge Haskins & Davey
Construction: Commercial Building Group

OLYMPIC PARK RAILWAY STATION

Development Manager: Olympic Co-ordination Authority
Architect: Hassell
Design Team: Ken Maher, Rodney Uren, Robin McInnes, Geoff Crowe, William Smart, John Woodman, Adrian Gotlieb, Andrew Cortese, Vanessa Yee, Mano Ponnambalam, Michele McSharry
Structural Engineer: Tierney and Partners
Services Engineer: Connell Wagner
Acoustic Engineer: RFA Acoustic Design
Landscape Architect: Hassell
Graphic Designer: Emery Vincent Design
BCA Consultant: Trevor Howse and Associates
Quantity Surveyor: Page Kirkland Partnership
Crowd Modelling Consultant: Arup Transportation
Fire Engineering Consultant: Stephen Grubits and Associates
Project Manager: Gutteridge Haskins and Davey
Construction: Leighton Contractors

SYDNEY INTERNATIONAL REGATTA CENTRE, ROWING SHEDS

Development Manager: Olympic Co-ordination Authority
Architect: Woods Bagot
Project Architect: Warwick Simmonds

Design Team: Warwick Simmonds, Phillippa Randall, Carl Degroot
Structural Engineer: Taylor Thomson and Whitting
Civil Engineer: Taylor Thomson and Whitting
Electrical Engineer: Barry Webb & Associates
Landscape Architect: Lorna Harrison Landscape Architect
Hydraulic Consultant: Thomson Kane
Environmental Management Planner: Connell Wagner
Quantity Surveyor: Page Kirkland Partnership
BCA Consultant: Philip Chun & Associates
Aerodynamic Consultant: VIPAC
Project Management: NSW Department of Public Works and Services
Construction: Abigroup

SYDNEY INTERNATIONAL REGATTA CENTRE, FINISH TOWER

Development Manager: Olympic Co-ordination Authority
Architect: Conybeare Morrison & Partners
Director in Charge: William Morrison
Project Architect: Janet Marsden
Design Architect: Terry Chin
Structural Engineer: Northrop Holmes Engineers
Civil Engineer: Northrop Holmes Engineers
Electrical Engineer: Flannigan Lawson Engineers
Mechanical Engineer: David Shreeve & Associates
Landscape Architect: Context Landscape Design
Design Brief Consultant: O'Hanlon Design
Hydraulic Consultants: Northrop Holmes Engineers
Building Regulations Consultant: Trevor R Howse & Associates
Interior Designer: Conybeare Morrison & Partners
Lighting Consultant: Flannigan Lawson Engineers
Acoustic Consultant: Robert Fitzell Acoustics
Services Consultant: Rust PPK
Quantity Surveyor: Q S Services, NSW Department of Public Works
Communications Consultant: Flannigan Lawson Engineers
Programming: P D M Management Services
Project Management: Department of Public Works and Services
Construction: Cooinda Constructions Australia
Steel Contractor: Torresan Engineers

PENRITH WHITEWATER STADIUM

Development Manager: Olympic Co-ordination Authority
Architect: Grose Bradley
Design Architect: James Grose
Project Architect: Sarah Kirkham
Documentation: Sarah Kirkham, Catherine Chesterman
Structural & Services Engineer: Pacific Power International
Landscape Architect: Lorna Harrison and Associates
BCA Consultant: Trevor Howse and Associates
OCA Development Manager: Peter Cowling
Project Management: Pacific Power International
Construction: D G Sundin and Co

SYDNEY INTERNATIONAL SHOOTING CENTRE

Development Manager: Olympic Co-ordination Authority
Architect: Group GSA
Design Manager: Edward Lynch
Project Manager: Jeffrey Klein
Project Architect: Brian Graham
Design Architect: John Andreas
Structural, Civil, and Services Engineering: Sinclair Knight Merz
Acoustic Engineer: ERM Mitchell McCotter
Landscape Architect: Spackman & Mossop
Environmental Manager: ERM Mitchell McCotter
Facility Access Consultant: Independent Living Centre
Cost Planner: Page Kirkland Partnership
Lighting Consultant: Barry Webb & Associates
Programming: Tracey Brunstrom & Hammond
Building Regulations: Trevor Howse & Associates
Project Management: NSW Department of Public Works and Services
Construction: Belmadar Constructions
Earthworks: Daracon

DUNCAN GRAY VELODROME

Development Manager: Olympic Co-ordination Authority
Architect: RyderSJPH (a consortium of Ryder Associates, SJPH Design Partnership)
Design Director: Paul Ryder
Project Director: Richard Dinham
Design Team: Ann Burton, Lucas Crabtree, Jaime Kleinert, Garth Davies, Michael Flynn, Sally Fitzpatrick, Kim Jones, Vivian Eardley, Paula Valsamis, Brad Sonter
Structural Engineer: Ove Arup & Partners
Civil Engineer: Ove Arup & Partners
Acoustic Engineer: Ove Arup & Partners
Hydraulic: Ove Arup & Partners
Geotechnical: Ove Arup & Partners
Traffic: Ove Arup & Partners
Crowd: Ove Arup & Partners
Fire Engineer: Ove Arup & Partners
Electrical, Mechanical, AOE, Communications & Lighting Engineer: Lincolne Scott Australia
Environmental Engineer: Advanced Environmental Concepts
ESD Master Planning: Eco Design Foundation Inc.
BCA Consultant: BCA Logic
Cost Planning: Rider Hunt Sydney
Cycle Track Consultant: R V Webb
Food & Beverage Consultant: Cini Little Australia
Landscape: Context Landscape Design
Project Management: Australian Pacific Projects
Construction: Walter Construction Group

SYDNEY INTERNATIONAL EQUESTRIAN CENTRE

Development Manager: Olympic Co-ordination Authority
Architect: Equus 2000 Architects; Joint Venture of Scott Carver, Timothy Court & Co, and SJPH Design Partnership
Design Directors: Stuart Scott and Timothy Court
Civil Engineer: Kinhill

Hydraulic Engineer: Kinhill

Electrical Engineer: Barry Webb & Associates

Mechanical Engineer: Lincolne Scott

Fire Engineer: Holmes Fire & Safety

Landscape Architect: Edaw (Aust.)

Quantity Surveyor: WT Partnership Australia

Environmental Consultant: Manidis Roberts

Project Management: Incoll Management

Construction: Lipman

SYDNEY SHOWGROUNDS EXHIBITION HALLS

Development Manager: Olympic Co-ordination Authority

Architect: Ancher Mortlock & Woolley

Design Director: Ken Woolley

Design Manager: Steve Thomas

Design Team: Dale Swan, Phil Baigent, Lynn Vlismas, Garry Wallace, Robin Yeap

Structural & Services Engineer: Ove Arup & Partners

Landscape Architect: Tract

ESD: Manidis Roberts

Acoustics PA: Arup Acoustics

Lifts: Roy Barry & Associates

Crowd Engineering: MacLennan-Almac Holmes

Building Regulations: Trevor Howse & Associates

Quantity Surveyors: Davis Langdon Beattie

Project Management: Australian Pacific Projects

Managing Contractors: John Holland Construction and Engineering

Construction: Thiess Contractors

SYDNEY SHOWGROUNDS MAIN SHOWRING

Development Manager: Olympic Co-ordination Authority

Architect: Cox Richardson, Peddle Thorp, and Conybeare Morrison (CPTC)

Structural Engineer: Hyder Consulting

Civil Engineer: Hughes Trueman Reinhold (HTR)

Electrical Engineer: Bassett Consulting Engineers

Mechanical Engineer: Bassett Consulting Engineers

Hydraulic Engineer: Hughes Trueman Reinhold (HTR)

Landscape Architects: Context Landscape Design

Lighting: Bassetts

Acoustic: Wilkinson Murray

Wind Studies: Professor Melbourne, Monash University

Communications: Bassetts

Environmental Consultant: Manidis Roberts

Traffic: Project Planning Associates

Quantity Surveyor: WT Partnership Australia

Building Certification: Philip Chun & Associates

Project Management: Australian Pacific Projects

Managing Contractors: John Holland Construction and Engineering

Construction: AW Edwards, Transfield, Concrete Constructions, Thiess

SYDNEY SHOWGROUNDS ANIMAL PAVILIONS

Development Manager: Olympic Co-ordination Authority

Architect: Pavilion Architects, a consortium of Scott Carver, SJPH Design Partnership, and Timothy Court & Co

Project Director: Richard Dinham

Design Director: Robert Perry

Structural/Civil Engineer: SCP Consulting

Structural/Mechanical Engineer (Building A - Sydney Indoor Sports Centre): Ove Arup & Partners

Structural Engineer (Building D 'Sprung Structure'): Miller Milston Ferris

Mechanical Engineer: Lincolne Scott Australia

Electrical Engineer: Barry Webb & Associates

Acoustic Engineer: Robert Fitzell Acoustics

Landscape Design: Context Landscape Design

Quantity Surveyor: WT Partnership Australia

ESD Consultants: Manidis Roberts

Mechanical/Environmental: Lincolne Scott

Fire & Safety Consultant: MacLennan-Almac Holmes Australasia

Waste Disposal/Hydraulic: Bruce Arundell & Partners

Traffic Consultant: Colston Budd Hunt & Twinney

Project Management: Australian Pacific Projects

Managing Contractor: John Holland Construction and Engineering

Construction: Baulderstone and Belmadar Constructions

HOMEBUSH BAY FERRY WHARF

Development Manager: Olympic Co-ordination Authority

Architect: Alexander Tzannes Associates

Design Director: Alexander Tzannes

Project Architects: Phillip Rossington, Louise Nettleton

Architectural Assistant: Andrew Tzannes

Structural Engineer: Taylor Lauder Bersten

Electrical Engineer: Carl Martin Associates

Landscape Architect: Sue Barnsley Design

Lighting Engineer: Carl Martin Associates

Graphic Design: Emery Vincent Design

Project Management: Gutteridge Haskins Davey

Contractor: Stage One: Australian Wharf & Bridge Constructions

Stage Two: Gledhill Constructions

STATE HOCKEY CENTRE

Development Manager: Olympic Co-ordination Authority

Architect: Ancher Mortlock & Woolley

Design Director: Ken Woolley

Design Manager: Dale Swan

Project Architect: Robin Yeap

Structural Engineer: Connell Wagner

Civil Engineer: RA Young & Associates

Mechanical/Electrical Engineer: Lincolne Scott

Hydraulic Engineer: The LHO Group

ESD Consultant: Manidis Roberts

Landscape: Tract

Acoustics PA: Arup Acoustics

Crowd Engineering: MacLennan-Almac Holmes

Building Regulations: Trevor Howse & Associates

Quantity Surveyors: Davis Langdon Beattie

Project Managment: Sinclair Knight Merz

Construction: Kell & Rigby and Abigroup

SYDNEY INTERNATIONAL ATHLETIC CENTRE

Architect: Philip Cox Richardson Taylor, and Peddle Thorp

Construction Manager: Civil & Civic (Lend Lease)

Structural Engineer: Connell Wagner

Civil Engineer: Ove Arup & Partners

Electrical Engineer: Barry Webb & Associates

Communications Engineer: Barry Webb & Associates

Mechanical Engineer: Norman Disney & Young

Landscape Architect: Belt Collins & Associates

Hydraulic Consultant: Ledingham Hensby Oxley & Partners

Acoustic Consultant: Louis Challis & Associates

Programming: Civil & Civic

Construction Manager: Civil & Civic

Quantity Surveyor: Civil & Civic

Traffic: Eugene Smith/BECA

Interior: Cox Nexus Design

Track and Field: Ray Young & Associates

Wind Studies: Professor Bill Melbourne, Monash University

Seating: Sebel Great Australian Seating

Structural Steel: Transfield

Prefinished Steel Products: Lysaghts

Paints: Taubmans

Concrete Masonry: Boral

Track: Balsam Pacific

SYDNEY INTERNATIONAL ARCHERY PARK

Development Manager: Olympic Co-ordination Authority

Architect: Stutchbury & Pape

Design Architect: Peter Stutchbury

Project Team Members: Fergus Scott, Ray Fitzgibbon, Katrina Julienne

Structural Consultant: The Structural Design Group

Electrical Engineer: Advanced Environmental Concepts

Hydraulic Engineer: ACOR

Landscape Architect: Phoebe Pape, Stutchbury and Pape

Lighting Consultant: Lincolne Scott

Environmental Consultant: Advanced Environmental Concepts

Quantity Surveyor: Page Kirkland Partnership

Project Management: NSW Department of Public Works and Services

Construction: Cooinda Construction Australia

Steel Fabricator: Austfab

NSW TENNIS CENTRE

Development Manager: Olympic Co-ordination Authority

Architects: Bligh Voller Nield

Design Director: Lawrence Nield

Project Director: Neil Hanson

Project Architect: Andrew Cortese

Project Team: Andrew Burges, Nameste Burrell, Graeme Butler, Kim Cameron, Catherine Chesterman, Hamilton Cue, Frank Ehrenberg, Bob Gardner, Mike Hale, Glenn Scott, John Whatmore

Interiors Team: Abbie Galvin, Russel Koskela, Damien Mulvihill

Structural, Civil, Electrical, Mechanical, Hydraulic, Fire & Acoustic Engineers: Ove Arup & Partners

Stadium Consultant: Building Design Partnership

Signage: Emery Vincent Design

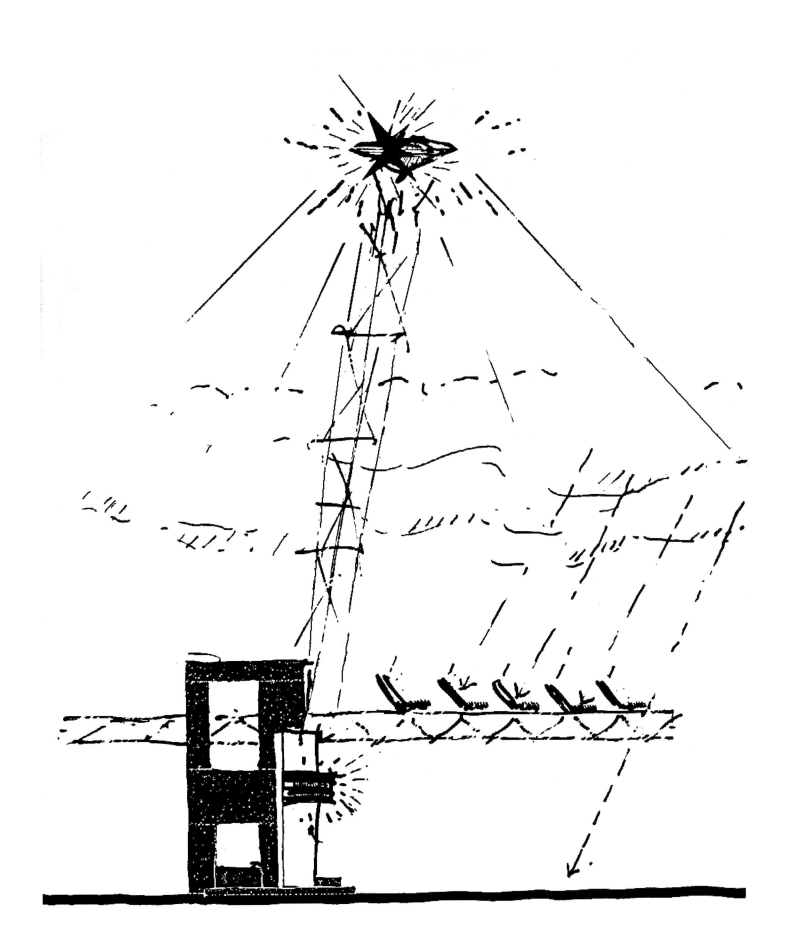

Access Consultant: Independent Living Centre
BCA Consultant: Stephen Grubits & Associates
Quantity Surveyor: WT Partnership Australia
Landscape Architect: Spackman & Mossop
Project Management: NSW Department of Public Works and Services
Construction: Abigroup
Sub-consultants: Pacific Steel, De Martin and Gasparini, Rescrete Industries, All Staff Airconditioning, Clipfit Glazing Systems, CVS Equipment, Venue Revenue Services, Spence Doors, Access Hardware, Fire Fighting Enterprises.
Suppliers: BHP, Pioneer Concrete, Hymix Concrete, CSR Emoleum

SYDNEY INTERNATIONAL AQUATIC CENTRE

Architect: Philip Cox Richardson Taylor, Peddle Thorp
Structural Engineer: Connell Wagner
Civil Engineer: Ove Arup & Partners
Electrical Engineer: Barry Webb & Associates
Mechanical Engineer: Norman Disney & Young
Hydraulic Engineer: Ledingham Hensby Oxley & Partners
Landscape Architect: Belt Collins & Associates
Lighting Consultant: Barry Webb & Associates
Acoustic Consultant: Louis Challis & Associates
Pool Filtration Consultant: Ove Arup & Partners
Corrosion and Condensation: Ove Arup & Partners
Wind Studies: Professor Bill Melbourne, Monash University
Communications: Barry Webb & Associates
Programming: Civil & Civic
Traffic: Eugene Smith/BECA
Quantity Surveyor: Civil & Civic
Tiler: Ace Ceramics
Glass & Aluminium Fabricators: G James
Project and Construction Management: Civil & Civic
Construction: Civil & Civic (Lend Lease)

SYDNEY INTERNATIONAL AQUATIC CENTRE OLYMPIC EXPANSION

Development Manager: Olympic Co-ordination Authority
Architect: Scott Carver
Structural/Civil Engineer: Connell Wagner
Electrical Engineer: Barry Webb & Associates
Mechanical Engineer: Lincolne Scott
Fire & Safety Consultant: Holmes Fire & Safety
Hydraulic Consultant:GJ Sparks & Partners
Landscape Consultant: Clouston
ESD Consultant: Manidis Roberts
BCA Consultant: Derek Hendry
Acoustic Consultant: Richard Heggie & Associates
Quantity Surveyor: WT Partnership Australia
Project Management: Sinclair Knight Merz
Construction: Leighton Contractors

NEWINGTON OLYMPIC VILLAGE APARTMENTS

Developer: Mirvac Lend Lease Village Consortium
Apartment Masterplan and Concept Design: HPA Architects with Bruce Eeles & Associates and Vote Associates

Design Development, Documentation and Administration: HPA Architects
Directors: P. Cotton, B. Eeles, P. Sinbandhit
Project Team Leader: K. Pappas
Project Architects: M. Weiner and M. Woollett
Project Team: R. Dabrowski, T. McKern, D. Jordan, S. Mitrovski, R. Pachon, O. Venevongsos, S. Hoskins, I. Parker
Interior Design: HPA Architects
Director: C. Rands
Designer: J. Warren
Structural Engineer: MPN Group
Project Management: Mirvac/Lend Lease
Construction: Mirvac Constructions - David Cracknell, Malcolm House, Glen House, Danny Visiatia, Warren Walters
Aluminium Windows: Micos
Concrete Pavers: Urbanstone
Ceramic Tiles: Ace Ceramics
Carpet: Mr Carpet
Kitchen Parquetry: Illawarra Floors
Ceilings: M & B Panzarino
Kitchen Joinery: IJF
Wardrobes & Joinery: Galliano
Development Managers: Mark Percy, Damien Carpenter

OLYMPIC SCHOOL

Development Manager: Department of Public Works & Services
Architects: Clare Design, Design Directors to the NSW Government Architect
Design Directors: Lindsay and Kerry Clare
Project Team: Department of Public Works & Services, Building Design Services
Structural Engineer: Department of Public Works & Services, Building Design Services
Electrical Engineer: Department of Public Works & Services, Building Design Services
Mechanical Engineer: Department of Public Works & Services, Building Design Services
Hydraulics Engineer: Department of Public Works & Services, Building Design Services
Environmental Design: Department of Public Works & Services, Environment and Energy Services
Hardware: Department of Public Works & Services, Building Design Services
Quantity Surveyor: Department of Public Works & Services, Building Design Services
Landscape: Department of Public Works & Services, Landscape Design Services
Project Management: Department of Public Works & Services, Sydney Region
Construction: Abigroup

SYDNEY SUPERDOME

Development Manager: Olympic Co-ordination Authority
Architect: Cox Richardson Architects & Planners
Sports Architects: Devine Deflon Yaeger
Civil Engineer: Taylor Thomson Whitting
Structural Engineer: Taylor Thomson Whitting
Services: Norman Disney Young

Geotechnical: Coffey & Partners
Fire Consultant: Holmes Fire & Safety
BCA Consultant: Derek Hendry
Environmental Consultant: Manidis Roberts
Acoustic: RFA Acoustic Design
Disability Access Consultant: Access Australia
Traffic: GM Burton Consulting
Quantity Surveyor: Page Kirkland Partnership
Food & Beverage: Food Service Design Australia
Interior: Total Event Experience
Construction: Abigroup

SYDNEY FOOTBALL STADIUM

Architect: Philip Cox Richardson Taylor
Civil Engineer: Ove Arup & Partners
Structural Engineer: Ove Arup & Partners
Mechanical Engineer: Addicoat, Hogarth & Wilson
Electrical Engineer: Civil & Civic
Communications: Civil & Civic
Hydraulics: Civil & Civic
Lifts: EPL
Planner: PCRTP
Acoustic: Peter Knowland & Associates
Interior: PCRTP
Quantity Surveyor: Civil & Civic
Landscape Architect: Landscan
Project Management: Civil & Civic
Construction: Civil & Civic

OLYMPIC SAILING SHORE BASE

Development Manager: Olympic Co-ordination Authority
Architect: Scott Carver
Design Director: Malcolm Carver
Maritime Consulting Engineer: Patterson Britton & Partners
Electrical Engineer: Barry Webb & Associates
Fire Engineer: Engineered Fire & Safety Solutions
Hydraulic Engineer: G J Sparks & Partners
Landscape: Edaw (Aust)
Quantity Surveyor: WT Partnership
Environmental Consultant: Woodward Clyde
Traffic Engineers: Colston Budd Hunt & Twinney
Project Management: Australian Pacific Projects
Construction (1998-99 Contract): St Hilliers

OLYMPIC SOFTBALL SPORTING FACILITIES,

Development Manager: Olympic Co-ordination Authority
Principal Design Consultant/Architects and Planners: Michael Davies Associates
Civil & Structural Engineer: Sinclair Knight Merz
Disability Access Consultant: Access Australia
Track & Field Consulting Engineer: Young Consulting Engineers
Electrical/Mechanical Engineer: Bassett Consulting Engineers
Hydraulic Consultant: Leddingham Hensby & Oxley
Landscape Consultant: Inside Out Landscape
Quantity Surveyor: Currie and Brown
Project Management: Incoll Group
Contractor: Haskins Contractors

RYDE AQUATIC LEISURE CENTRE

Development Manager: Olympic Co-ordination Authority
Architects/Masterplanning: Peddle Thorp & Walker and Donovan Payne Architects Joint Venture
Joint Venture Directors: John Bilmon, Carl Payne, Kim Donovan
Project Leader: Kurt Wagner
Project Design: Brian Moore
Design Management: Peddle Thorp & Walker
Leisure/Operational Management: RMP & Associates
Structure/Hydraulics/Civil Engineer: Hughes Trueman Reinhold
Pool Hydraulics/Filtration: Geoff Ninnes Fong & Partners
Electrical/Mechanical/Acoustics Engineer: Basset Consulting Engineers
Landscape Architect: Site Image
Cost Planning: Rawlinsons
BCA: Philip Chun & Associates
Project Management: Australian Pacific Projects
Construction: John Holland Constructions

HOMEBUSH BAY NOVOTEL IBIS HOTEL

Development Manager: Olympic Co-ordination Authority
Architect: Travis McEwen Group
Acoustic Engineer: Renzo Tonin & Associates
Structural Engineer: Connell Wagner
Services Engineer: Donnelley Simpson Cleary
Landscape Architect: Belt Collins Australia
Interior Designer: Forbes & Harris
Planner/Urban Designer: Ingham Planning
Traffic Engineer: Colston Budd Hunt and Twiney
Access Consultants: Access Australia
Building Certifier: Stephen Grubits & Associates
Project Management: Lend Lease Projects
Construction: Lend Lease Projects

OLYMPIC CO-ORDINATION AUTHORITY

David Richmond (Director General)
Bob Leece (Deputy Director General and Executive Director, Development)
Mick O'Brien (Executive Director, Operations)
Bob Adby (Executive Director, Finance)
David Pettigrew (Executive Director, Government and Environment Co-ordination)
John Kent
Dianne Leeson
Dick Prince
Paul Gilbertson
Greg McTaggart
Stuart McCreery
Geoff Fogarty
Jim Stone

PUBLIC ART ADVISORY COMMITTEE

Leon Paroissien (Chair)
Juliana Engberg
Chris Johnson
Joanna Capon
Lawrence Nield
Wendy McCarthy
Peter Emmett

DESIGN REVIEW PANEL

Chris Johnson (Chair)
Catherine Bull
Leon Paroissen
Michael Keniger
Laurence Nield
Wendy McCarthy
Paul Reid
Neville Quarry

OCA URBAN DESIGN GROUP

Bridget Smyth (Director)
Anne Loxley (Public Art Co-ordinator)
Katie Perry (Asst Public Art Co-ordinator)
Mike Horne
Lee Andrews
Charlotte Gay
Myra Karasik
Sharon Francis
Sarah Pearson
Daniela Romeo
Glenn Allen
Lindsay Turner
Lucy Creagh
Robin Simpson
Michelle Cramer

ARCHITECTS, LANDSCAPE ARCHITECTS, URBAN DESIGNERS, ARTISTS AND COLLABORATORS:

IN THE SHADOW
Artist: Janet Laurence
Technical Advisor: Jisuk Han

Project Management: Ley Reynolds (WWP), Tony Edwards (DPWS)
OCA Development: Stuart McCreery, Geoff Fogarty
Consultants: Maunsells, Barry Webb and Associates, Sydney Fountains,
Construction: Abigroup

OSMOSIS
Artist: Ari Purhonen
Technical Advisor: Hargreaves Associates
Project Management: Ley Reynolds, Wilde and Woollard Pacific
OCA Development: Jim Stone
Consultants: Ove Arup & Partners, Barry Webb and Associates
Construction: Abigroup

RELAY
Artist: Paul Carter, Ruark Lewis
Technical Advisor: Hargreaves Associates, Kate Luckraft (CADD), DPWS (CADD)
Project Management: Richard Fechner, Vince Joseph
OCA Development: Dick Prince, Jim Stone
Consultant: Ove Arup & Partners
Construction: Abigroup
Stonemason: McMurtries

LUMINOUS THRESHOLD
Artist: James Carpenter, Richard Kress
Project Management: Ley Reynolds, Wilde and Woollard
OCA Development: John Kent
Consultants: Taylor Thomson Whitting, Barry Webb and Associates, Sydney Fountains

5000 CALLS
Artist: David Chesworth and Sonia Leber
Technical Advisor: Nigel Frayne, Resonant Designs
Project Management: Greg McTaggart, OCA
Construction: Multiplex

OVERFLOW
Artist: Peter Cripps and Terri Bird
Design Advisor: OCA/ Hargreaves Associates
Technical Advice: International Conservation Services
Project Management: Ley Reynolds, Wilde and Woollard Pacific

FEATHERS AND SKIES
Artist: Neil Dawson
Technical Advisor: Hargreaves Associates
Project Management: Multiplex
OCA Development: Colin Ging, Peter Lacey

LOST AND FOUND
Artist: Elizabeth Gower
Technical Advisor: Cox Richardson
Project Management: Abigroup
OCA Development: Paul Gilbertson
Construction: Abigroup

Index

ACKNOWLEDGEMENTS   This book has been produced over a period of almost three years, and it was only the total dedication of the photographer and author, Patrick Bingham-Hall, that pushed it through to completion.

Along the way, we received encouragement from many people, in particular David Richmond, Director General of the Olympic Co-ordination Authority and Chris Johnson, Government Architect NSW.

Patrick Bingham-Hall wishes to express his sincere thanks to Graham Ford, John Cloran, Antoinette Lee, Penny Bingham-Hall, Rick Turchini, Warwick Simmonds, Philip Cox, Janet Roderick, Fiona Martin, John Eglinton, John Seligman, Michele Fleming, John Baker, Bruce Eeles, Margot Riley, Annie Tennant, Kate Stewart, Charlotte Gay, Davina Jackson, Heidi Dokulil, James Grose, Ken Woolley, Gloria Myer, Janet Laurence, Neil Durbach, Camilla Block, Peter Stutchbury, Mike Horne, John Barnao, Andrew Andersons, Ed Obiala, Lee Price, Samantha Biggs, Jenny Crawford and Kath Tonkin for their specific help and support.

So many architects gave so freely of their time in sourcing sketches, plans, elevations and sections for inclusion, that to try to remember them all here runs the risk of a serious omission. To all of them, we say a sincere thank you.